Shale Boom, Shale Bust:
The Myth of Saudi America

DAN DICKER

Table of Contents

Introduction

I was watching my screens on Thanksgiving Day, 2014—a day I would normally rest my monitors. Even though the markets were closed, I was getting an indication on the electronic premarkets of just how bad the next day's short Friday session was going to be for oil stocks. The electronic market for oil futures was trading, even as the floor exchange was closed for the holiday, and the numbers I saw were just flat-out breathtaking: oil was down more than $6 dollars a barrel.

Wait, what? I kept looking at the screen in absolute disbelief: *this is just crazy*, I kept thinking, *just crazy*.

I knew what the reason for this amazing collapse of oil prices was, or at least what the headline would be: *OPEC leaders meeting in Vienna have not been able to agree on a cartel-wide production cut—members' quotas will stay high*. Going into the meeting, oil prices had been in a free-fall since August, dropping more than $20 a barrel to below $80. Some analysts had predicted that OPEC would take the opportunity of their yearly meeting to shore up prices by dropping production targets.

But I didn't, and I didn't know anybody else with half a brain in oil who believed we'd see a cut. In the weeks leading up to the meetings, Saudi Arabia, the controlling power in OPEC, had indicated that there was very little chance of an agreement in Vienna. The day before the meetings, I had been on Bloomberg television, assuring Trish Regan that no agreement was at all likely; the Saudis had not gotten nearly what they wanted from other OPEC members nor the markets to approve that move in November.

I said all of this as I was still clinging to a fairly substantial long position in oil futures, a position I had been "rolling" (moving from month to month) for more than 3 years and making a fairly nice steady profit from. Believe me, if I had thought that the lack of an OPEC production cut would cause such a concurrent massive cut in the trading price of oil, I would have been out of that position several days prior to my appearance and the outcome of the OPEC meetings. I believed completely that a production cut default was already "in the market"—i.e., that prices were already representing that miss at the meetings. Instead, prices now began a secondary collapse below $80 that would ultimately land at $40 a barrel.

I knew that the conventional wisdom on the drop in oil prices was going to be ascribed solely to this move by the Saudis, a conclusion that was far too simple to explain the massive collapse. No, something else, something even more important was going on…and as my losses rolled up and my margin calls rolled in, I had many compelling reasons to figure it out.

The Saudi reticence to cut production was just a catalyst, I realized days later. The bigger theme was an already overdue bust that was happening in U.S. shale oil. Hydraulic fracturing (or fracking) of shale was a technology initially designed to tease natural gas from where it was hiding inside rock. However, in recent years, the process had been modified to release oil, and a bonanza of new oil production had been having unprecedented success here in the U.S. The rapid production growth from perhaps half a dozen shale formations had truly revitalized U.S. oil as if the clock had been turned back to the start of the first domestic oil boom of the 1920s.

Exploration and production had absolutely exploded in three main shale "plays": the Williston basin, whose U.S. area in the Dakotas was more commonly known as the Bakken; in a band running through Southeastern Texas named the Eagle Ford shale; and in another Texas area further west, the Permian basin. These three shale plays, along with half a dozen smaller ones, had almost doubled U.S. oil production, from under 5 million barrels a day to more than 9 million barrels by early 2015. Fracking of shale to release oil has been so successful, in fact, that it has eclipsed domestic fracking for natural gas in importance here in the U.S. To be very clear, when I refer to shale, both in the title and remainder of this book, it should be understood that I am always talking about *oil*.

But this oil bonanza, as it was now being shown to me, had been built on a house of cards, ready at any moment to topple over. The list of fragile flaws in the system was long. Each state had its own set of regulations and oversights on leases and operations, with no consistent framework for oil shale fracking. Despite (or because of) the complete freedom in oversight, fracking for oil from shale had grown at a frightening and undisciplined pace. As prices declined, it became clear that much of this breakneck activity had been financed by very risky and highly leveraged capital investments that mirrored some of the worst pyramiding schemes I had ever seen. But because prices had been high, many of the shortcomings had been conveniently overlooked: oil was being taken out of the ground as quickly as it could be drilled. This rapid growth in production from shale had completely overwhelmed the current pipeline network. Where pipes didn't exist, a completely new business of transporting oil by rail began to emerge, adding cost but even more danger from spills and exploding rail cars. Perhaps most shameful was the rampant burning of associated natural gas from those same wells where oil was coming but no gas pipelines yet existed—a practice known as *flaring*. Oil companies were simply unwilling to wait or pay for the proper infrastructure to be built for associated gas. Oil was pricey, whereas gas was not. The cheaper natural gas was being wasted, simply burned up at the wellhead, in favor of the more-profitable shale oil.

All of this new oil was saturating the appetites of domestic refiners at the closest nexus points to its production, and conventional storage was almost completely full, yet the drumbeat for the building of the Keystone pipeline and its added supply of Canadian tar sands oil continued to get louder, for no practical reason. In response to all this new supply and the planned increases to come, the state regulatory bodies, Washington and the industry itself—instead of concentrating on better fracking standards, the building of capable infrastructure, or a more responsible and restrained pace of production—put most of their efforts on repealing a long-standing ban on the export of domestic oil, thinking global market access would cure every ill. I knew that its repeal, if it were granted, would only lead to even faster drilling and draining of this very limited resource.

The months following the OPEC announcement showed me just how rickety the entire structure for retrieving shale oil had become. Oil companies that had been the darlings of Wall Street not one year earlier were now losing 70-80% of their share value, as their corporate bonds, which were already poorly rated, risked complete default. Virtually every company involved in shale production was forced to slash development budgets, hoping to ride out what they prayed was a temporary dip in the price of oil. Yet projected production numbers from all of these players continued to rise, almost insuring that prices would stay cheap. What had been a universally optimistic industry not 6 months prior had changed overnight into a frightened group playing a collective game of chicken, as oil producers hunkered down with reduced budgets and hoped like mad that the "other guy" would go broke first.

That shale oil had folded like a cheap suitcase so quickly and completely was incredible to witness and, I thought, incredibly important: it was undeniable proof that as a nation, we had completely bolloxed this once-in-a-lifetime opportunity.

During the boom from 2010-2014, the promises of shale oil were fantastic. As U.S. oil companies rushed headlong into shale production, larger integrated companies outside the United States were stepping on and over each other to gain some partnership or joint-venture piece of the rapidly shrinking U.S. shale pie. Resource 'experts' were quick to point to the shale revolution to claim the end of 'peak oil'—the idea that fossil fuels were a resource quickly running dry—and claim that another 100 years lay between us and a time when we'd have to consider using something else to power our lives. Economists heralded a new U.S. industrial renaissance, believing that the newly flooding domestic energy from shale oil would bring back factories and middle-class jobs lost to Asia in the last two decades. Washington crowed how shale oil would ensure the energy independence of the United States, but it also proposed using shale oil as a political weapon to be wielded on global markets in the fight against oil-rich and oil-dependent enemies alike. Collectively, these ideas had birthed a promise of "Saudi America"—where the U.S. would dominate global energy in the same way it currently dominates the world economically and militarily.

All of those promises now lay shattered as half of the rigs drilling for shale were suddenly turned off, thousands of jobs were lost, and U.S. oil companies battled for their lives.

To me, this was more than a story of another boom/bust cycle in the oil patch. God knows that the oil business had seen enough of those already and knew what they were about. But I saw shale oil not as just another in a long line of boom/bust cycles in U.S. oil production, but as the last boom we were likely to have. I didn't see shale oil as just another technological advance in a long line of advances yet to come; I saw it as the last best chance to put the U.S. on a firm footing towards a cogent national energy policy and as a conduit towards a real and necessary renewable energy future. And we were blowing it.

But I didn't see these mistakes as irreversible. Instead, I saw the bust in shale oil as a chance to get it right. I truly believe that shale can deliver on many, if not all, of the promises it has already pledged.

In the coming pages, I devote a lot of time and energy to the reasons for the recent decline in oil prices, and I predict that the next boom, as inevitable as I think it is, will not materialize quickly. That is a prediction, but it is also a hope: only a very long period of lower energy prices can bring the wholesale reorganization that will be needed to sweep the control of these very precious assets from the most irresponsible and weakest hands into those with the financial ability to withstand natural market cycles and plan much further ahead. From the oil industry, a long down cycle will move shale oil production from those with a 10-month planning horizon to those with a more appropriate 10-year horizon. Further, our government needs to use this very short time of lower energy prices to prepare national standards and initiatives to allow the next coming boom in shale to finally deliver on its many promises. For those of you who are reading this book to gain investment ideas, you shouldn't be disappointed: I devote quite a bit of time on predicting what the landscape of this new U.S. energy world might look like and the likely winners and losers from this reorganization.

Simple economic laws would say that this period of low prices can't really last very long, no matter what I believe the industry needs. As costs for exploration continue to rise, so does the global appetite for oil—two simple facts that ensure that prices must substantially rise again.

But my hope is that in this brief window of low prices, we might find some clarity. The "bust" cycle in shale since late 2014 spotlights the deficits in how we're managing shale oil in a way that the "boom" cycle between 2010 and 2014 as oil averaged above $90 a barrel cannot: with oil prices high, focus centers on quick growth, quick profits, and soaring share prices. But with oil prices low and energy companies reeling, there is a brief window for reflection—to try and understand what is happening and why it is happening and to chart a more responsible and less purely opportunistic way to a smarter, more sustainable energy future.

My 30-year perspective as a trader, analyst, and columnist gives, I think, a unique view into these questions—totally without ulterior motive for financial gain, yet with an inside understanding of the oil business and the financial markets that guide that industry. I hope to help you understand shale oil's boom and current bust and why the hopes and hypes of shale need to be reimagined and restructured...before oil prices recover and the markets again give a green light to energy companies to resume their natural instinct—of pissing it all away.

Let's start our search for a better understanding of the shale oil opportunity by exploding the biggest conceptual myth surrounding it: the idea of the United States becoming a global energy power equal to those we know in the Middle East. This idea has been stylishly dubbed "Saudi America."

Chapter 1:

SAUDI AMERICA

Ah, Saudi America: A modern dream of an energy-independent United States, free from the dependency of foreign oil and the reliance on U.S. foreign policy to sustain its flow.

Let's look at it. Figures 1-1 and 1-2 are two charts I love, courtesy of the U.S. Energy Information Administration.

Figure 1-1:
The Growth of U.S. Dry Shale Gas Production

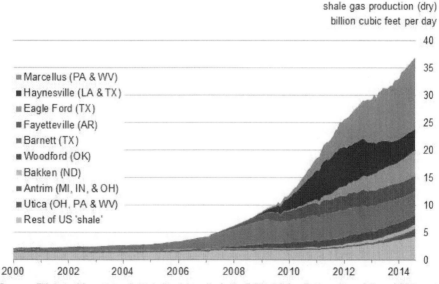

Sources: EIA derived from state administrative data collected by DrillingInfo Inc. Data are through August 2014 and represent EIA's official shale gas estimates, but are not survey data. State abbreviations indicate primary state(s).

Figure 1-2:
The Growth of U.S. Tight Oil Production

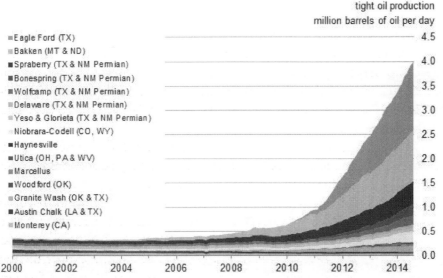

Sources: EIA derived from state administrative data collected by DrillingInfo Inc. Data are through August 2014 and represent EIA's official tight oil estimates, but are not survey data. State abbreviations indicate primary state(s).

I adore these charts because they represent so well the dream of Saudi America: a seemingly never-ending, straight-upwards trajectory in production of both oil and gas here in the U.S. Just looking at these two charts, you'd certainly conclude that America was on the verge of not only overtaking everyone else on the planet as the number-one producer of fossil fuels, but also ripe to become, for the first time in its history, a world-leading exporter of the soon-to-appear excess of fossil fuels that these charts imply.

Indeed, that's the very common 'wisdom' I have encountered in my media roles over the past few years, often expressed by pundits working outside of the energy sphere. In early 2014, Thomas Friedman of *The New York Times* advocated for the export of U.S. oil, arguing our excess could crater global prices and help in our now fairly sticky 'relations' with Russia. In Chapter 4, I argue against the logic of a full-scale rollback of the U.S. oil export ban, but the point Mr. Friedman makes is about our imminent national energy largesse—and its ability to be wielded as a new and powerful political weapon.

If only it were true.

Saudi America Is a Myth

Saudi America is, in fact, a myth—or at least half of one. Only one of those two beautiful charts I showed you at the start of this chapter is real: the one that shows a true trend of increasing and sustainable production—in natural gas. The other, in oil reserves particularly from newly developed shale plays, is just a temporary joke being played on the U.S. public and on many in Washington. It is merely a phantom, showing a future of energy independence that might materialize only for the very short term of a few years, before retreating once again from whence it came, into oblivion.

Oil from shale is not going to make the U.S. sustainably independent of foreign imports, *ever.* Moreover, the more successful it becomes, the more likely it is to erode as a significant energy source quickly, far more quickly than many judge it will. Far from being a political weapon for export, oil from shale is only another energy boom cycle that has already made a few very fortunate oilmen and shareholders very rich, but is destined to disappoint the economy as a whole and consumers here at home as an energy savior, as the amount that is produced begins to rapidly level off and then shrink… sometime within the next half decade.

Let's figure out why.

"Unconventional oil" refers to any produced barrels that are not retrieved using the most traditional methods of the last 100-plus years. Most people's typical image of oil production involves a wooden derrick with gushing black gold spewing from the top, perhaps with a grizzled John Huston-like rig worker poised beneath it, dancing. (*We've hit a gusher, fellas! We're gonna be rich!*)

Figure 1-3:
The Beginning of Oil Production, in 1901

This photo of Spindletop, Texas in 1901, shown in Figure 1-3, heralded the beginning of U.S. oil production, and there is still a significant amount of 'un-enhanced' production that remains in the United States, where the pressure of underground veins of crude is more than enough to send significant volumes to the surface for capture and transport. But this simple and cheap era of crude exploration continues to decline in the U.S.: it provided under 2 million barrels a day from the total 9 million barrels of late 2014 daily production. For years, the decreasing numbers of conventional production were thought to doom the United States into forever being a consumer of imported oil, at the mercy of Middle Eastern sheiks and always on the brink of an energy crisis that would rival the long gas lines and recession that accompanied the OPEC embargo of the 1970s.

And then the shale revolution in oil took off in 2009.

You could go to any number of books or read several hundred articles on the process of extracting oil and natural gas from shale and the process's creator, the recently passed George Mitchell. I won't bother with the tale here, other than to lay out the simplest basics of the process. Throughout the United States (and in a few other choice areas around the globe) are striated rock formations of shale that have captured fossil fuel deposits within them. Extricating these oil veins requires a drill bit and an escape route that first moves vertically downward into these shale layers; then, the extraction process moves horizontally, which is when water and other 'fracking fluid' chemicals are injected to stimulate the rock and release the captured oil and gas. Not only does the age of these formations have to be nearly perfect to attempt this process, but so does the relative strength of the rock, the surrounding rock and soil composition, the depth of the relative layers, and dozens more variables you'd need to be a geologist to name.

All of this perfection delivering economic potential to shale occurs far less often around the globe than you might think. Although China and Russia are often mentioned as two countries with potential reserves equal to or greater than the U.S., recent data suggests that neither has the underground composition to make shale oil economically recoverable at all, at least using current technology. Outside of the U.S., only Argentina and Venezuela have shale formations worthy of wide-scale exploration, yet neither is anywhere near the scale that the United States enjoys. In this way, Saudi America is an apt description.

That's the first point about Saudi America that you need to keep in the back of your mind: U.S. shale formations in half a dozen plays throughout our country represent a very unique and limited resource globally. Further, what the United States does with these resources is a once-in-a-millennium opportunity that very few other nations will share.

Further, the ability to access this windfall was only a result of the unique technological capabilities of U.S. geologists and engineers. Score one for the good ol' U. S. of A. What has spurred the rapid growth of this new source of good-paying jobs and a revitalized oil and gas sector (and related materials and services industries) has been a confluence of those two very unique factors: the innovations here in the United States of horizontal drilling and hydraulic fracturing technologies combined with a number of absolutely perfectly formed shale formations. Together, they have created the perfect conditions for liftoff of this revolutionary energy source ready to yield lots of super-fine quality crude oil at a relatively cheap price.

Cheap Shale?

But how cheap is cheap? Oil prices will have an obvious connection to production costs, and there is an equally obvious fundamental balance between those costs and the demand. Let's look at the demand side of this equation before getting to price.

One way I like to think of the world demand for oil is to imagine a very large bowl or empty tureen, representing current global daily demand. The job of oil companies is to fill that bowl every day and be prepared to refill it again the next day as it empties. As all of the varied types of oil production from all over the globe come together to add their contributions into our daily demand tureen, they all will try to first contribute the cheapest oil they can: cheaper oil delivers higher margins and better profits. Believe it or not, there are many supply sources for oil around the world that can be accessed for as little as $5 a barrel. At the other extreme, there are supplies that could be developed today with a breakeven cost of more than $140 a barrel.

Figure 1-4:
Breakeven Costs per Barrel by Production Area

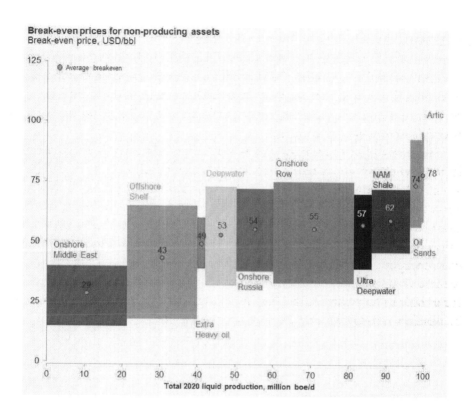

Break-even prices for non-producing assets
Break-even price, USD/bbl

Figure 1-4 is a chart that's important to consider, even if it isn't entirely comprehensive. It shows some of the more prevalent conventional and unconventional oil sources and their average breakeven cost. It doesn't explain all the economics going on in the oil patch, but it's a good start to understanding the relative values of various sources. The important point to remember right now is *not* the average breakeven point of any particular area (even shale—don't jump the story, please), but the wide spread of costs up and down for each. Although the average cost is often quoted, the high and low boundaries of production costs are much, much more important.

Particularly for understanding the possibilities for "Saudi America," one even more important thing from this chart should be understood: the expense of producing shale oil. U.S. shale oil is hardly the cheapest oil source out there. In fact, shale has several competitors in cost efficiency, including many other non-conventional oil sources. Indeed, North American (NAM) shale is eclipsed only by oil sands and arctic reserves as the most expensive non-conventional oil to produce. There is a very wide spread of production costs in shale oil, so this one chart cannot and should not serve to condemn shale oil as a mostly uneconomic oil source at all. To the contrary, efficiencies in horizontal drilling techniques have been improving on these breakeven costs at a rapid pace, and some of the shale producers have better margins than even some remaining conventional resources. Further, there are obvious core areas for shale drilling that are far more cost effective than others, and I could spend a lifetime (or another book) outlining the most prolific of these. But for our purposes, be aware that oil derived, for example, in the Williston Basin of the Bakken in North Dakota could have a $30 breakeven price as easily as a $75 breakeven price. I simply want you to remember that just because we are talking about shale oil does not mean that we're necessarily talking about cheap oil. In some places, it could be very expensive to find and source.

Now let's go back to our needy tureen—because ultimately, this demand analogy I'm using will be the basis for the rest of our discussion on price.

Let's say that the world needs 90 million barrels of oil every day. To fill our tureen on any given Tuesday or Thursday, we'll access all the oil we can which comes out of the ground most cheaply—which starts almost exclusively from supplies from OPEC members, some of which (for example, the Saudi Ghawar oil field) have been spewing oil for pennies for decades since the 1950s. Costs for these barrels could be as low as $3, or maybe as high as $20. That's super for them: profits for OPEC members will always be the greatest in any oil environment. OK, once OPEC and its members have decided how much to add to our pot and how much not to add (the calculus of this is a story of its own), we'll scour the globe for other conventional supplies, oil that requires little more than we saw in that first picture of Spindletop. Some of them we'll find in Africa, some in Venezuela, some in Mexico, some in the U.S. and elsewhere. We've still not raised our breakeven cost much, so perhaps we're still pumping oil and filling our demand bowl for less than $30 a barrel. We move on, perhaps with nearly half of our tureen accounted for, and fill up with some choice, mostly shallow offshore barrels, then move on to Russian supplies, as you can see: you can read the chart as well as I can.

Somewhere along the line, as we're getting closer to filling up our tureen, we're going to have some choices to make. We'll get to a point where we're left with a deficit of several million barrels a day that we'll need to fully satisfy the world's demand, and several places we can go to get those barrels. There are very complicated deep-water projects we can undertake, or we can brave the very harsh conditions of the Russian (or American) Arctic, or we can endure the added production and processing costs of oil sands mining, or we can go to less efficient areas in the U.S. shale plays. For now, let's not talk about what choices we're going to make or why.

Just for now, let's understand how those choices oil companies make — just as the tureen is being fully charged—impact the most important factor of price. As we close in on completely filling our tureen, we're going to have to pay a higher and higher price for those barrels, because we've run out of the cheap ones now. Indeed, the most expensive barrel we'll have to buy will precisely be the *last* barrel we'll need. This is where the idea of 'marginal barrels' comes in: these are the last few barrels that must be produced in order to satisfy global demand—and they are by definition the most expensive.

What might not be clear yet is that the market price we'll have to pay for *all* the oil that we've just used to fill our tureen is *at least* as much as the cost for that last barrel we've used to fill it. Think about that for a second. Despite the fact that most of our oil has costs that are exceedingly cheap, the need for a single market price won't let us buy oil cheaply. It might be fair and we would certainly like to have a sliding market price for every single barrel of oil based on its individual cost. We'd like to have a standardized *profit margin* – maybe add $15 a barrel, and pay $20 a barrel to the producer of $5 oil and pay $60 to the producer of $45 oil. But the market doesn't work that way. Markets set only one standardized price, and we still must incentivize the producer of every barrel to continue to supply us with that one price.

It's clear that the most important producer that we need to incentivize is the producer of our marginal barrels. If they do not make a profit, they will stop making them available to us and we will inevitably run into a shortage of oil supply. What happens in a market where there is a shortage of supply? That's right, the price goes up, until the incentive is returned to our marginal producer of crude oil. The price to produce marginal barrels to fill out global demand is the most important in setting the price for oil everywhere.

We'll talk a lot about markets and marginal barrels—who has them, who can produce them, and who should. But a few further observations should be pointed out here. First, marginal barrels are the last into the tureen, but not necessarily the first out; the oil market does not work as cleanly as that. Those quick adjustments are left to what are called "swing barrels," which have often referred to Saudi or other supplies of oil production that could be easily added or subtracted to the global supply chain. *Swing barrels* can be used to defend market prices or to keep prices stabilized, should the owners of these swing barrels decide to use them that way. But marginal barrels can become swing barrels, should someone like the Saudis decide that they're suddenly uninterested in protecting price or the stability of price. Marginal barrels then become swing barrels as the most expensive barrels and the most cost sensitive, and indeed are going to be the first forced out of the tureen—a perfect action of direct economic forces.

Have I confused you yet?

Finally, and this may be the most important point, it should be clear that although some U.S. shale barrels could be cast in the role of marginal barrels and could then find themselves in the role of swing barrels, Saudi oil or other OPEC nation barrels cannot: they can only take on the role of swing barrels, because of their very low cost of recovery. Further, although they might take on the role of swing barrels, it would be entirely and only at their discretion and choice.

We have made a case in this section that the U.S. has so many of the amazing and unique qualifications to be and indeed has become, a major global energy producer—again. We have seen that shale oil is an opportunity that few other countries will enjoy. Even if they do find some shale assets in China or Russia, it is almost sure that they won't present on anywhere near the scale they have presented to us here in the U.S. The incredible opportunity of shale combined with American technological know-how and quick drilling has unleashed a vast new supply of high-quality oil. This has driven many to gush that the United States is not just a competitor to the Middle East as a producer of energy, but a superior to them. Indeed, when the U.S. surpassed everyone else in the world in its total production of oil and gas in 2014, the idea of Saudi America really seemed to have come true. If you're bigger than Saudi Arabia, aren't you also better?

But price of production and the role of U.S. barrels as marginal barrels destroys any hope of being a competitive 'winner' to the Saudis. Because

U.S. shale can never truly compete on price with Saudi barrels, U.S. shale barrels will also never avoid the risk of becoming swing barrels. Shale is just far more price sensitive than OPEC oil.

This is why the United States can never live up to the hype of "Saudi America" and why the idea of true U.S. energy independence from the Middle East is a hopeless myth. If American shale oil is always at risk of becoming a marginal barrel, then the market ultimately decides whether it will be produced, and how much of it can be produced. Creating a target whereby U.S. production undermines or completely cuts out dependency on foreign oil is a misguided effort of illogical economics. Therefore, unfortunately, the United States will never truly live up to the hype of the term "Saudi America."

We've determined that U.S. shale oil producers are currently more likely to be forced into the unenviable guise of 'swing barrel' producers, now that oil prices are low and OPEC has shown an increasing willingness to abandon the role, at least temporarily. Because of this, it's more important than ever to understand the economics of shale oil producers. Unfortunately, the economics are pretty scary—and have less in common with other business models that build enterprise value and more with pyramiding schemes. See the next chapter.

Chapter 2:

SHALE OIL IS A
PONZI SCHEME

Shale oil is a Ponzi scheme. I don't mean that there is a vast conspiracy inside the energy world to confuse investors about its potential or fleece Wall Street. No, I mean that the business of drilling for oil from shale creates an endless circular appetite for more drilling for lesser returns. Think of a classic Ponzi investment scheme: constant fresh capital is needed to generate the false gains and pay off early investors. Shale production is similar in that more and more drilling is constantly needed to continue to generate even *equivalent* returns, much less growing ones. In a classic Ponzi scheme, when the new money inevitably stops coming in, the pyramid quickly collapses. In shale, that moment when the pyramid becomes too heavy to sustain itself is far from being reached, but the inevitability of it is equally clear. Further, I believe that the tipping point is far closer than most other analysts and certainly the Energy Information Administration (EIA) believe it to be.

The returns from shale might be far more real than in a classic Ponzi scheme, where there are no real returns on capital, only a pyramiding of new investment to pay off the old ones. But the ultimate trajectory of investment in shale will end up being shockingly similar, in my view: the earliest investors will reap the majority of the rewards, while the late investors will be left with decaying wells that are unable to service the increasing amount of debt needed to drill for them.

The main reason I characterize shale oil production as a Ponzi scheme is because of the fast decay of shale oil wells as compared to virtually all other oil production. One chart is enough to give a good indication of the progress and problems of oil from shale—see Figure 2-1.

Figure 2-1:
Shale Well Decay Rates

Average oil production per well during the first 48 months of operation
barrels per day

Here we have a compilation by the EIA for production of the average well in the Eagle Ford shale in East Texas, but it serves well as a model for shale oil in general. Two very interesting points should be immediately clear:

1. the rate at which oil comes out of freshly drilled wells has improved every year in the last five years since 2009, and

2. the amount of oil that shale wells deliver is substantially front-loaded: more than 50% of all the oil you will see from a shale well is recovered in the first two years, and the greatest proportion of that will appear in the first 6 months.

Fantastic improvements in drilling technology have improved well results, as we can see. And while those improvements have made initial results from wells ever more exciting, they have also sharpened the fast speed at which wells deteriorate. Big initial results breed enthusiasm and expectations of continuing success that cannot happen, but I'll return to that idea later. For now, let's talk a little more in depth about the second point, regarding the front-loaded nature of shale.

ABC Oil Joins in the Shale (Ponzi) Game

Let's try and make this easier by starting from scratch: let's imagine a start-up shale oil company. Our company—let's call it ABC oil—has no capital of its own, and for the sake of our model, ABC needs to borrow every dime it can to get it up and running producing oil. Fortunately, that's no problem, because financing for good acreage shale projects has been pretty easy to find in the last five years, with lots of investment capital chasing high and very profitable oil prices. Let's say ABC manages to find and sign leases for good acreage on or near other prime acreage that has been delivering solid drilling results for other, bigger oil companies. Financing through bond offerings at 'regular' high yield levels results in a 5-7% rate. This might sound like a lot, but is actually very, very good and only possible in a Fed-inspired zero interest rate environment. Such low rates for relatively "junky" B- to CCC-rated paper have been one of the many reasons for the whirlwind development of U.S. shale since 2010.

OK, now let's drill a well. Imagine that the drilling costs to completion will total about $10 million from start to finish and will take about a year to complete and start giving us oil. So we have to burn some cash during that year, while rig operators and crews are hired, but no problem, we expected this. At 8 or 9 months, we're getting close to completion, and the results of our drilling are becoming clear. And let's say, for simplicity's sake, that we have a winner project, a well that will deliver at least an average amount of oil for a well in the Eagle Ford shale, like we see represented in the chart above.

Great! Oil starts coming out of our lone company well, and although we have to pay transport costs and perhaps other minor processing, we're able to book an excellent return of $80 a barrel—this from an oil market that is trading on the Chicago Mercantile exchange for about $100 for most of the years from 2010-2014. In the first three months at this price, we'll book more than $2 million (300b/d x 90 days x $80/barrel). Super! We've paid our debt for the previous year ($10m x 7% = $700,000), and we now have cash in the bank to pay all of our obligation the next year coming. With these out of the way, the next three months are even better, even if the production numbers start to slip a little towards month six. We'll book perhaps another $1.5 million, enough to either pay down some of our initial debt, or sink some cash into the next well we're planning on developing, or give back some profits to early investors or officers of our fledgling company. Early success with our first well has made financing for the next one even easier,

24

and we'll likely not bother to retire debt that's not due for a decade or more. We're ready to start on the next well, developing it really close to the first and hoping for similar results. As we continue to drill wells very near to the spot where we put our first well, we'll likely see very similar results and very similar economics. Excellent money will flow initially from these wells, which will deliver money for the next project.

But here's the point: If we're in the shale business, there is going to be a constant need to develop the next project. This is not because the wells aren't exciting and profitable—it's because they are *almost immediately* exciting and profitable. Our biggest profits are overwhelmingly going to be in the first few months. And when our first well's production numbers get reported, that initial good 60 days of production is all we'll need to inspire more investment and financing to keep us moving forward. Wall Street has shown a particular bias towards oil companies that can demonstrate two things: potential recoverable reserves and production increases. This is true for any oil company, no matter where they concentrate. But shale players can generate enormous initial returns based on these two metrics, compared to just about everyone else. The EIA and the success of surrounding players in shale have taken good care in generating lots of enthusiasm towards the amount of oil likely held underground: we've heard nothing but the potential reserves inside the 'hot' shale plays—the Eagle Ford particularly, the Permian formation in West Texas including the Spraberry and Wolfcamp, the Californian Monterey shale, the Bakken of the Dakotas, and others. And as to increasing production, that requires only one very big thing: more and more successful wells.

Let's go back to ABC's first well: what were the final results of our fledgling well? Certainly as time moved along, the production numbers continued to slide, and by year 3, the well is hardly delivering much cash flow at all. The overall results for our first well are still very profitable, but they're no longer very impressive. In 3 years, though, averaging 150 barrels a day, our well has generated a profit of almost $13 million. That's not bad at all: we've seen a 30% investment rate of return (IRR) in three years. But the first six months of profits made that well look so much more promising. No matter to us, at least in terms of our plans going forward and our continuing need for more and more spending to generate more and more new production. We've long ago forgotten about our first well because we're focused on the next dozen that we're at various stages of progress on instead. ABC oil has become a 'hot' shale player.

Meanwhile, debt inside the company continues to accumulate as wells continue to be completed. Moreover, we haven't once talked about what can go wrong. Clearly, we could have gotten close to completion on any of our wells and found out that our project was going to deliver far less oil than the average we were counting on. (To be fair, we could also have gotten far luckier than the average numbers.) We could have chosen the wrong frack formula for our particular drill site. We could have a sudden increase in drilling costs for any number of reasons, a dispute from the landowner or the town, an environmental issue, or some problem with the pipeline company we're working with.

But clearly, the biggest problem we could encounter in becoming a hot shale producer in one of the hot shale plays would be a sudden drop in the price of oil. With shale oil companies, the need for continuing drilling activity makes them most vulnerable to a downward price cycle. A 20% drop in oil will equally drop returns by 20% and alter the economics of every well, pushing forward our projected payoff times and cutting our cash flow, which drives everything else, including our crucial exploration budget.

Call for Financial Oil Insurance

Of course, ABC oil isn't run by stupid, unaware people. It knows very well that the worst thing that could happen to it is a sudden drop in the price of oil. And it has taken some steps to mitigate those risks by hedging into the financial futures markets.

Despite having spent my career in the oil futures market, I've avoided a deep discussion of them in this book, and I won't start here. If you're looking for a deep dive into the workings of energy futures, I refer you to my previous book, *Oil's Endless Bid*. For now, let's simply refer to oil futures as a viable commercial hedging process—think of it as an insurance policy for ABC oil, on the possibility of rapidly dropping oil prices. ABC is smart and ready to engage in the futures markets and pay for some of that insurance. So what's the problem?

Hedging in the futures markets is very expensive indeed, and is more restrictive than just owning "insurance." Using the futures market implies a willingness to lock in a final price for production: for example, if you sell oil in March of 2011 for delivery in March of 2012 at $97, you are going to sell it for that price at that time. Further, if you're locking in at any price, you're obligated to receive that price, no matter what the markets do in the meantime. That means that if you're hedged and the market goes down in the interim, you're going to realize a better price when you're finally ready to put your oil on the market. But it also means that if you're hedged and the market goes up, you're going to receive less. This brings some difficult choices, even if you're willing to spend the money for your financial "insurance policy."

Primarily, you've got to ask: How much of your production are you willing to hedge—and lock in your final price? If you hedge 100% of your future production—a move that would help guarantee your future economics— your problems are hardly solved. With 100% of your production hedged, if the market absolutely tanks and drops 20%, 30%, or 50%, you will look like a hero and your shareholders will nominate you for another year or three as the company CEO (and won't complain when you give yourself a $15 million bonus). On the other hand, if you hedge it all and the market rallies, you've got a lot of explaining to do as your competitors lap you in their financial results. Finally, if you hedge all of your future production and the price of oil stays relatively stable, as it mostly has from 2012-2014, you've just spent quite a lot of money for insurance that proved to be totally unnecessary—and a big nasty write-off for all to question in your quarterly reports. Remember that just about every oil analyst is telling you that oil is far more likely to rally than it is to drop, and the prospects over the long term are for oil prices that are not just higher, but spectacularly so.

What do you do? Well, if you're like most oil companies in the shale business, you do hedge your production, but not all of it. In fact, if you're the average shale oil company, you've only hedged around 35% of your next year's production, and less than 15% of your production two years out. (This is according to a research note by RBC, analyzing the amount of hedging done for 2014 and 2015 production as of November 2014.)

This relatively small level of safety taken on by most of the oil companies working in the big shale plays actually makes a lot of intuitive sense. Why should you risk losing out on the potential of a very, very strong crude rally and the enormous profits that will come with it for the sake of a negative possibility that almost no one believes will happen? Sure, you might take out some insurance on some of your barrels, but you wouldn't risk your job or the possibility of that "big score" that delivers terrific results, screaming share prices, and huge stock options—and certainly not if nobody else seems to be doing it either.

And overwhelmingly, that is what happened in shale. (As an aside, there are some conservative players who did hedge more: Devon, for example, had 80% of its shale production hedged before the 2014 crash. Apache, as an example of the extreme opposite pose, did not hedge its 2014 production at all.) The point I'm leading to is that, on balance, access to the financial markets hasn't altered the sensitivity of shale oil players to the market much.

But let's get back to ABC oil. It's working hard to add wells to its portfolio, continue to post great production results, and excite investors to buy its stock and subscribe to its latest bond offerings. Spending is increasing, but on balance, its debt-to-EBITDA ratio is manageable and not frightening anyone. Yes, it is going to have a problem if oil prices suddenly tank, but ABC is as well-hedged as everyone else and no more at risk—at least that's what its managers tell themselves.

It's All Good (Until It's Not......)

Finally, ABC gets another great shot in the arm (besides the good results the company is already getting with its drilling): initial production numbers are going up. That's the second part of Figure 2-1 at the beginning of this chapter that I said I'd come back to. Whereas before ABC might see 300 barrels a day in the first 3 months of well production, now numbers are increasing 20% or more every year. Better fracking materials, better methods in drilling techniques and seismic imaging improvements are increasing efficiency, along with better spacing between wells, better trained crews, all dropping the netback time (which is how long before a well breaks even) and increasing the total production from each well.

Wow! This is great news for everyone in the shale fracking business. The EIA is increasing its estimates of recoverable reserves for everyone, enthusiasm is nearly frantic, and investors are now beating down your doors to be a part of your fledgling company. If you hit on all cylinders at once, maybe ABC oil becomes a rocket story like Athlon Energy, a newcomer into the Permian shale of West Texas that went public in August 2013 for $27.50 and saw its stock soar in a year to over $60, only to be bought by Encana energy for $7.1B in September of 2014, an equivalent of $71 a share. The boom times in shale were certainly exhilarating and addictive.

With all of this good news—increasing initial results from better technology and vast increases in projected reserves—how can I possibly be calling the shale oil revolution a Ponzi scheme? The rapid growth of someone like Athlon has been repeated dozens of times in the last 4 years, and increases in initial production results in every year since 2009 has made a very strong case for the ultimate longer-term potential of shale oil. And on first glance, I'll admit it sure does look that way. Certainly, the EIA thinks it's true: the EIA believes not only that vast improvements in efficiencies can be interpolated almost forever, but also that the production numbers from shale can be repeated throughout the plays and not just through a very, very thin slice of the prime areas of those plays, all of which are being feverishly over-worked already (see Figure 2-2).

Figure 2-2:
North American Oil Production Potential
(Historic and Projected)

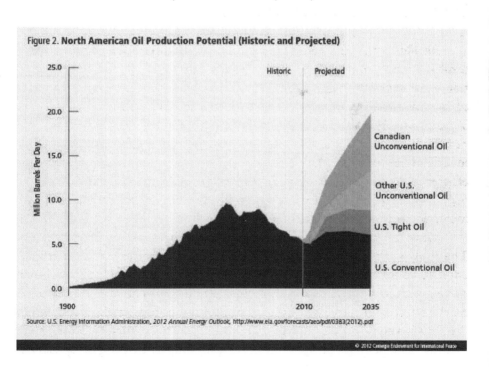

Figure 2. **North American Oil Production Potential (Historic and Projected)**

Source: U.S. Energy Information Administration, *2012 Annual Energy Outlook*, http://www.eia.gov/forecasts/aeo/pdf/0383(2012).pdf

© 2012 Carnegie Endowment for International Peace

Not only does the EIA believe in the continued ramping up of tight oil production well into the next decade, it is even convinced of the potential of increasing efficiencies on conventional supplies here in the U.S., which have done nothing but *decrease* since the 1970s. This is a fantasy swallowed whole by Wall Street and U.S. investors. No, despite all the good news, shale is still inevitably headed for a production cliff. It's just well shrouded and tougher to see as the boom times are going on.

But let's look a bit further into the future, remove some of the shrouds, and expose the real truth: there are only a few core areas in shale worth working here in the U.S., and they're all being relentlessly tapped right now. In Chapter 4, I'll go into more depth about those areas and why we are really looking at a much more limited resource in shale oil than we think we have. Mark Papa, the ex-CEO of EOG Resources, one of the premier shale producers, remarked on his exit that all of the even potentially good shale plays here in the United States have already been entirely picked over. What we are seeing in production here is the outcome of the best technology and best-capitalized players in the global oil industry drilling in the richest and greatest potential acreage that this country has to offer.

But what's inevitable is that efficiency and technological advances in drilling for shale oil cannot make up for the ultimate deficiency of prime acreage. When the potential of technology is reached, the fundamentals of just how much good shale acreage there is out there will really begin to be felt. What cannot be seen clearly now, is that this "great acreage" is actually very limited indeed. In fact, I believe we may have already reached the peak of its production.

Let's circle back to ABC oil to try and make this point. ABC has come a little late to the shale game, so perhaps its working acreage is not quite as prime as perhaps Hess's or Continental Resources.' Still, ABC has had very good results for its first several wells, which, remember, were selected precisely because they were most likely to deliver really good results. But as ABC matures and the months and years go on, ABC will move to drill new wells further and further outside those super-prime areas that the company initially highlighted. And new results from those wells outside its core areas will be weaker.

Even though ABC was an upstart and small, that truth of ultimately "using up prime acreage and moving on" is true of everyone in the shale business, big or small—while some companies have tremendous portfolios of unexplored acreage that could see them do fantastically well for a decade or more, there are dozens of smaller companies on the margins that are working their best acreage right now. Some of them, like Rosetta Resources (ROSE) and Halcon Resources (HK), are arguably working them not to be viable production companies, but to look good solely as takeover targets—their futures are shrouded, but inevitably bleak. And even the largest companies that have years of prime acreage to drill will inevitably find a need to move into less productive areas at some point—although investors need not worry about that prospect anytime soon. Here's my point, and the reason I use so diabolical a reference that conjures up images of Madoff-type fraud: it is clear that U.S. shale oil cannot continue to progress in production in the way it is being interpolated by the EIA and the oil industry.

Beware of Oft-Quoted Shale Oil Predictions

Front-loading of shale production is one reason I think shale oil has some of the attributes of a Ponzi scheme—inspiring increased capital injections based on very exciting initial results that cannot be maintained. Interpolating the progress of U.S. oil production based on the massive success shale is having right now and believing those spectacular numbers can be sustained for decades is another.

Ultimately, and far sooner than most analysts believe, U.S. shale production will consist of ever less productive wells that cost more to drill, take longer to pay themselves off, and generate less oil. The EIA believes that nothing like that will occur for at least the next 25 years. I think that the peak of U.S. shale potential will be reached in the next 10, if it hasn't been reached already. Once that peak is realized, the pyramid will begin to fall apart—and quickly.

This is why I characterize shale oil using such an obnoxious term; it is not just to incite interest and book sales. The full potential of U.S. shale oil reserves is a debate that I tackle in Chapter 4. Right now, it looks limitless, but it's not. The advances in drilling strategies and fracking technology has also increased the outer limits of shale's potential. But where those limits actually lie is ultimately irrelevant.

I know that oil is limited, and that every well, whether fracked or not, ultimately decays to zero. But shale is different from every other kind of

SHALE BOOM_ SHALE BUST

oil-procurement technique. Shale wells get used up at a rate almost 10 times faster than other oil projects and therefore force shale oil producers into constantly chasing more activity in successively less and less promising acreage, to just stay even. That is entirely unique for shale. In order to actually grow, shale oil companies need an absolutely furious pace of investment and drilling, paying off early investors and bondholders, attracting new investors, and spending ever more capital. That outline for continued success sounds familiar in many ways to me.

It sounds like shale oil has a lot in common with a Ponzi scheme. Let's bring forward this idea of shale as a special case in oil production in the next chapter, where we talk about scalability, which really matters if we were hoping for the U.S. to become oil independent because of shale. It also really matters if we are to figure out who the major winners and losers of the current bust and the coming next boom will be.

Chapter 3:

SHALE SCALABILITY
AND RESULTS

We know what the breakeven costs are for oil, not only for conventional wells, but also for shale wells working in every different play and part of each play. We know the breakeven costs of getting oil from offshore wells in 800 feet of water as opposed to those in more than 2 miles of water. We know the breakeven costs almost down to the dime for nearly every well that's being drilled today. That makes the economics of oil relatively easy to gauge, at least as oil goes down in price, as it has been doing for the last half of 2014, as shown in Figure 3-1.

Figure 3-1:
Citibank Analysis of Breakeven Shale Well Prices

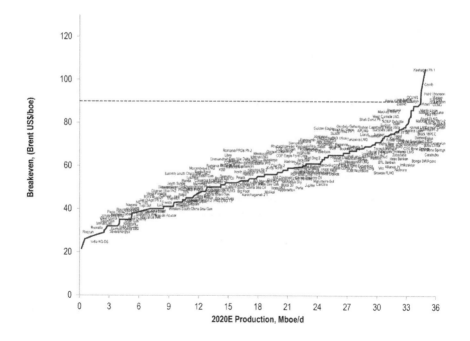

It is clear that a lot of oil doesn't come out of the ground under $70 a barrel. And the fact that a lot of it does come out of the ground a lot more cheaply than that doesn't really matter. We've already talked (in Chapter 1) about the marginal barrel of oil, and how that one last barrel that fills demand can set the price for virtually every other. If you have a demand for 92 million barrels of oil a day, it is the breakeven price of the most expensive one you need to produce that will set the fundamental cost for every other barrel, no matter how cheaply the rest of them are produced.

Nobody will work to produce oil that loses money in the open market. And if even one barrel of oil that is produced isn't profitable, it will ultimately disappear from the supply chain. That seems fairly obvious. With oil prices of around $50 a barrel, at least 9 million barrels a day of production is uneconomic. That's equally obviously unsustainable. So why are production numbers continuing to increase here in the U.S. through 2015, and how are oil companies surviving so far?

What has 'saved' production from immediately falling off a cliff has been two mixed blessings for the oil industry: the long-term scheduling of production and financial hedging.

The "Long Game" for Oil Companies

No oil project starts on a dime. From the moment that a site is targeted to the time when oil finally is first retrieved is immensely variable dependent on where you're drilling. For a deep-water offshore project, that calendar can stretch for 3 to 5 years; for a shale well, it can be as short as 6 to 8 months. Because of the relatively short time commitment and the fast decay rate of horizontally drilled wells, shale is now considered to be by far the most 'scalable' of oil resources.

Scalability of shale is the most important reason the U.S. will never fully realize oil energy independence.

If you're a major oil company like BP or Chevron and have committed $3 billion or more to a deep-water project, there is little you can do in adjusting to fast-changing market prices. Once that deep a financial commitment has been made over that long a period of time, you are compelled to move towards full production for the life of the well, which should produce strong volumes for at least 6 years and usually much more. Even if prices for one year or two remain challenging, you will bank that over the life of the well, it will show a profit; it is impossibly risky to abandon sunk costs even during the earliest stages of development, no matter what else happens. Contracts are signed for years of commitments of services on drilling logistics and consulting, cementing, pipes, safety, and transport. There is the long-term rig—floater or jack-up to be contracted—the several teams of workers, and the logistics for servicing that rigs needs for food, water, and medicine. All this and more needs to be carefully planned for years into the future. In short, off-shore production is one of the least scalable sources of oil in the world.

In contrast, for shale oil, the game is a lot faster and far more 'shoestring.' The crews for any single well can be as few as a handful of full-time workers, with many of the services companies only needing part-time access to a particular well. There is no need to contract a specialized drilling rig that can cost $50,000 to $650,000 a day for a five-year term, as with an off-shore project. Total cost for drilling an average shale well can easily remain under $10 million. Wells are fast to spud (i.e., deliver oil for the first time) and fast to decline, with an overall decay rate of more than 30% a year, as opposed to the industry average of 5% a year. That means that new wells need to be planned for and drilled all the time if shale companies are to stay even on production numbers or increase them to continue to attract financing and increase share prices. High-risk bonds have been the source of most of that financing, and the pace of shale growth and the appetite of the bond market in the U.S. has moved that drilling quickly into less and less fertile acreage.

This is the life facing a marginal U.S. shale producer. The plus side of this equation for the shale players are the costs and commitment: perhaps $10-15 million to sink a well with the vast majority of the oil gone in the first two years. In the shale game, you have to drill when the drilling's good, and the well life will not allow you to 'ride out' a negative market anywhere near as easily as you can if you're one of the 'big boys' working in multi-billion-dollar projects.

Therefore, shale players are going to be the quickest producers to react to dropping crude prices—not because they *want* to be, but because they *have* to be. The difference in production scheduling will force their hands, where it simply won't for others producing oil from other types of wells. But one further financial move can save many of these shale players from immediate contraction, as we've discussed a bit before: hedging in the futures and forwards markets.

Financial Hedging

Let's talk in a bit more detail about hedging as it will give us more insight as to which shale players will thrive and prosper as the current bust cycle moves into the inevitable new boom. Many of the shale players have been wise enough to use the futures markets to hedge at least a modicum of their production in 2014, an absolute savior to them as oil prices collapsed.

For example, Newfield Exploration is an oil company that would be considered a marginal player in shale and would be compelled to make a quick production adjustment because of low prices. Instead, Newfield will skate happily away from its peers during this oil price crisis because of hedges it made. It smartly hedged more than 80% of its production through 2016 at about $90 a barrel. In contrast, Apache and Whiting Petroleum have almost no hedges in place and will likely have to change their plans more quickly in light of lower realized prices. As proof, Whiting attempted unsuccessfully to find a buyer in early 2015 because of its weak capital position.

Continental Resources looked unbeatable during the oil collapse. It was well positioned with hedges before its CEO Harold Hamm decided that oil had gotten low enough at $83 dollars a barrel. Believing that oil was unsustainable below $80, Hamm bought them all back; now Continental is relatively unprotected as oil swoons in the $50s. But Continental is hardly alone. RBC has estimated that only 14% of 2015 production of U.S. shale oil has been hedged in the futures market, and for 2016, the numbers are significantly worse than that. If those numbers are right, hedging in the futures market won't save the shale players from making some very tough decisions in 2015 and 2016.

The dire conditions of oil companies that have limited hedges and therefore need to make some very fast and panicked moves to recapitalize is a theme that is running through the industry in 2015. The reason it's particularly important for producers of shale oil is because of shale's scalability—its need to react most quickly to changes in the price of oil. In late 2014, I was on Bloomberg Television with Alix Steel, a reporter I've worked with for years at thestreet.com before she was wisely lifted from there by Bloomberg TV. We talked about shale oil and scalability.

"You're not going to put $17 million into a shale well and just walk away?" she asked. "You're going to want to generate some cash flow for the money you've already invested, right?"

Yes, of course she was right—about a well that you've perhaps spudded in August of 2014 as prices have just started to decline. At the moment you started drilling, all was well: oil prices were seemingly rock steady at $100 a barrel. But these few wells, which started right before the collapse of oil prices, represent only very few of what's out there producing. When we talk about scalability and the relatively quick adjustments the shale producers need to make, we're talking about wells that have already been in operation for 2 years or more, others that have only begun work, and finally those wells that are being targeted but haven't yet had dime one spent on them.

So, when we talk about this kind of scalability, what exactly gets scaled back? To start, the latest well projects that were merely in planning stages or initial geological survey modes aren't going to happen: these are the first ideas to be cut and relate directly to the capital expenditure drops inside oil companies that are being planned. Companies also won't be drilling many new wells this year, or they will lower the number they had previously planned on. Then, there are the wells that have been in service for more than 2 years: perhaps 80% or more of the recoverable oil has already been drained from these. As a total package, oil companies can cut all of these old and newly planned projects rather easily without adjusting production levels much, if they can increase the rates and efficiencies on what's left. And finally, there are those wells that are just beginning to eat up capital. If you're not obligated to develop these sites (as some leases require), you can abandon them while returning at a more opportune market moment. All of this—i.e., the 'easy' adjustments to your drilling schedule—can be restructured in a matter of weeks.

Now, *that's* scalability. That's also a lot of work, perhaps more than half of what you've been doing or planning on doing that won't get done and won't immediately affect your bottom-line production numbers. But try doing that for deep-water or oil sands production—you simply can't. But look more closely: what have you actually done? According to the projections from the shale oil producers during quarterly reports for 2015, you haven't cut production at all, while you have magically cut your spending—in some cases by as much as 70%. That sounds like a fantastic recipe to get your profitability and your stock price up in a hurry while surviving a swoon in oil prices. But that's hardly what happened in the spring of 2015.

No one is really fooled by these new "tricks" of the books, least of all Wall Street. The real truth is, as a producer, cutting spends while maintaining production is only putting off the hangman's noose of cratering oil prices and revenues for the time being. What you're actually left with is a smaller portfolio of assets that are now producing at breakneck speed, decaying far faster than you originally planned, with few new assets coming on line to take their place in the future. At some point, you're going to need the barrels from those wells you've shut down prematurely and particularly the barrels from the wells you've put off developing.

What's most important is that there will be an enormous brick wall of dropping production for your company (and the entire shale oil industry, in fact) that you're going to slam into down the road. Somewhere, those assets you've been relying on to get you through the hard times are going to decay—with nothing to take their place. You can hope to restart what you've deferred to develop when your production begins to plummet, and that's likely the plan of many shale players for 2015, but the more important question is: when the wall hits, will they be able to ramp up again, and ramp up again in time to avoid disaster?

Remember, shale is sensitive to price not because it wants to be, but because it has to be. So while shale players are learning how to cut back during a down cycle, they've not yet learned or planned how to make it to the next upcycle when markets allow you to restart the spigots again. The boom is so new and the bust in oil prices so unexpected that most shale players had no plan for cratering markets. In 2015, most of them are playing it totally by ear, and many will have disastrous results for their lack of foresight. For now, however, shale oil's compulsion to start and stop production based on market price makes it by far the most sensitive oil source to crude prices around—far more than offshore oil and still more than oil sands recovery, the two other sources that they need because of high costs to be sensitive to crude prices.

So this is one of the biggest points about U.S. shale oil that the crude collapse of 2014 has made clear: because U.S. shale is easily scalable and needs, for its survival, to be sensitive to crude prices and because OPEC and Saudi Arabia have recently chosen to give up their historic role as global swing producer, U.S. shale barrels have been forced to replace OPEC and particularly Saudi crude as 'swing barrels' inside the global supply chain. In other words, the market determines the future of shale production more than every other kind of oil production. Put another way, shale oil has become the "LIFO" (last in, first out) source for oil for our imaginary tureen analogy we used in Chapter 1 on Saudi America. When demand cycles increase or supplies drain low, the U.S. shale industry now sits there with the quickest tap to twist on. But when producers get "too enthusiastic" about oil prices and supplies glut, or when economics compress global demand, or when renewables partially displace fossil fuels, it will be the U.S. shale producer who will be forced to cut back.

Now it's easier to see why the United States will have a much more difficult road to being energy independent: you can't rely on U.S. shale to get you there. No matter whether the oil market stays depressed for three months or three more years, the production numbers for the U.S. won't ever be stable enough to make the United States independent of foreign oil. Only a consistently and reliably high market price can do that, something that the oil bust of 2014 proved is still hardly guaranteed. U.S. shale oil is first in line to be the supply source that must contract when the market demands it.

The myth of U.S. energy independence (or at least crude oil independence from foreign producers) is confirmed by the economics of the technological breakthrough that was supposed to deliver that dream of Saudi America to us all: horizontal fracking of shale.

Many of the largest producers of shale oil in the United States believe that they have found the solution to being the newly born, but unhappy, 'swing producer,' entirely at the whim of the oil markets—an end to the U.S. export ban. Although this prohibition to transport domestic crude oil overseas does have terrific arguments for its repeal, it is hardly a solution to the continued promise of 'Saudi America.' The next chapter explains why an end to the U.S. oil export ban is hardly the silver bullet that U.S. oil companies claim it to be.

Chapter 4:

THE U.S. EXPORT BAN ON OIL

Some energy policies were actually borne out of good intentions and not just as reactions to rapacious instincts. One of these was the crude oil export ban put in place in the United States during the 1970s. But the trajectory of this export ban and the effect of it today has created a perhaps unintended but useful restriction on American oil barrels reaching global markets.

The export ban on domestic crude oil was borne out of the Arab-Israeli war of 1973, but it was not only the support of Arab combatants that brought about the OPEC ban of oil to Western nations. Negotiations on oil rights from U.S. oil companies working inside OPEC nations had reached a tipping point where many Arab states were ready to finally fight back against the weak margins they had been receiving for their own natural resources. In short, the OPEC cartel was beginning to understand the power of the oil barrel that it held, and it used the 1973 war as a convenient reason to put that power to the test.

It was incredibly effective. Long lines to the gas pumps were only one very memorable effect of the boycott, but a full-scale recession for the U.S. economy was the scary possibility that forced the Nixon administration into some very quick negotiations with OPEC, including the end of a stabilized oil price that U.S. oil companies were delivering and U.S. consumers were enjoying at the pumps. And although the OPEC embargo inexorably linked U.S. energy policy to Israel, it also ended an insouciance of U.S. oil companies to Arab national resources that has never returned. Significantly, the OPEC embargo was also the start of a really free-floating price for global crude. Several new energy policies were established as a result of the embargo after it ended in 1974, including incentives to revitalize U.S. drilling for crude, a new Strategic Petroleum Reserve (SPR), the 55-mile per hour speed limit, and what I'm discussing in this chapter: a new export ban on domestically produced crude oil.

Taken in the context of the aftermath of such a destabilizing economic event as the 1973 OPEC boycott, you'd look upon the U.S. export ban as a very, very good idea: retaining resources at home in a moment when U.S.

production was significantly on the wane. What production that was likely to develop at the time was under little danger of any negative margin or profitability compared to barrels being imported from overseas. These were very dear resources with easy access to domestic markets, including a fresh outlet to fill newly built SPR tanks.

Fast-forward 40 years.

Oil production is booming here in the United States, courtesy of new technologies in shale fracturing, unleashing oil in areas once thought already run completely dry during the time of the Nixon Administration. Today, current estimates of recoverable oil from the Eagle Ford shale play in Mid-Texas run as high as 10 billion barrels. Optimists in the West Texas Permian basin have been heard at times touting three times that. With more than 9 million barrels a day of domestic production, U.S. crude imports are now under 50% of demand, really for the first time in modern history. As to the remaining U.S. oil demand that is imported, Canada has taken over the top slot from Saudi Arabia, with all indications that Mexico and Brazil are moving to quickly unleash their domestic production potential in the next several years. Now when the U.S. imports oil, it overwhelmingly comes from friends and not supporters of our enemies. Not only is U.S. dependence on 'unreliable' Arab sources waning, but OPEC's ability to apply political pressure to the United States using the spigot has weakened as well.

But all of this good news has one bad spin for domestic producers of crude. Even though, on balance, the U.S. still imports a good percentage of oil from overseas, there has developed a real supply glut of domestic oil in those areas where drilling and production is moving at a breakneck pace, particularly in Texas. Transport costs can make it more economical to import Rotterdam crude to an East Coast refinery than to contract for West Texas crude to arrive by rail. These simple economics have had a negative impact on the producers in the red hot shale production areas: crude prices for the Bakken and more recently for the Permian basin have languished at significant discounts to West Texas Intermediate crude (the U.S. financial benchmark) as well as other basis prices. For example, look at the difference in prices between Bakken oil blend and Louisiana Light Sweet oil, as quoted at one of the U.S.'s largest refinery hubs on the Gulf Coast (source: Platts):

Figure 4-1:
Comparison of the Price of Bakken Oil and Louisiana
Light Sweet (LLS) Oil

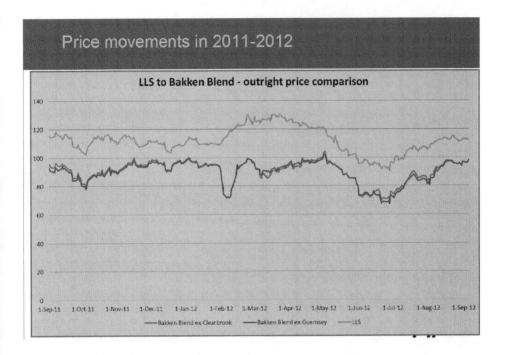

Although $7-8 discounts have been common, $20 discounts have not been unusual to see. In the West Texas Permian basin, crude generally prices closely to Midland WTI, with that discount to Cushing WTI reaching more than $10 a barrel in the last year.

Figure 4-2:
WTI vs. Midland (Permian) Crude

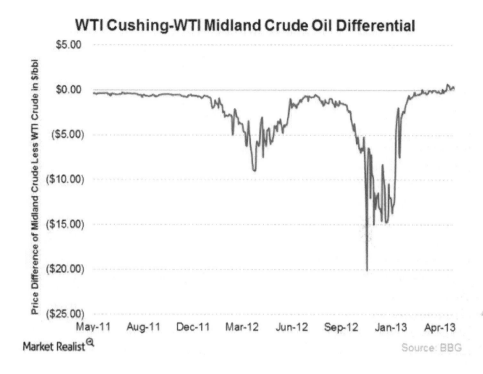

WTI Cushing-WTI Midland Crude Oil Differential

Market Realist

Source: BBG

The explosion of crude transport by rail has helped to stabilize some of these differentials more recently in 2013 and 2014, but further discounting is still a major worry for crude producers in the hot shale plays of West Texas and North Dakota, especially when their shareholders are banking on further rapid increases of drilled wells. However, even if crude by rail has taken up much of the recent slack, many believe that rail transport will soon reach its limit, and, not counting the increased risks that rail transport of crude poses, there remains no guarantee of a further rapid increase of pipelines or other infrastructure to carry the stuff away.

U.S. Crude Oil Prices Lag the World

To make matters worse, U.S. financial benchmarks for crude have been running at least at a $5-a-barrel discount to global benchmarks, with $15 discounts not uncommon: see Figure 4-3.

Figure 4-3:
West Texas Intermediate (WTI) vs. Brent Oil Spread

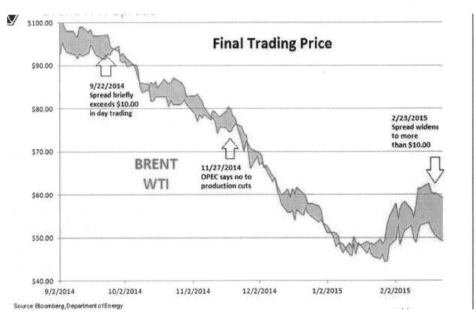

Pioneer Natural Resources has a unique presence in the Eagle Ford and particularly the Wolfcamp region of the Permian. Imagine if a producer like Pioneer were realizing in 2012-2014 an $85 or perhaps $90 per barrel price for its crude, while producers everywhere else on the globe were easily commanding closer to $110 a barrel (or more) for grades of more sulphurous crude not nearly as valuable as the high-quality sweet barrels Pioneer is generating. It would, I admit, be maddening; if you were Scott Sheffield, the CEO at Pioneer Natural, you would certainly speak up and make your outrage public about an export ban that seems entirely anti-business and anachronistic. It would be tremendously frustrating when the product you're marketing is delivering a $15-$25 more a barrel premium in the global marketplace, with only a 40-year-old outdated law standing in the way.

44

And your argument for access to that marketplace would be a logical and sound one indeed. Refined products from oil (gasoline, heating oil, jet fuel, etc.) have never been subject to any export ban, with gasoline exports reaching an all-time high in 2013. Neither have other U.S.-produced commodities ever been subject to any export ban, including coal, wheat, soybeans, lumber, cotton, pigs' feet, or any other you can name (with the interesting exception of natural gas). With other commodity producers free to explore the global marketplace for the best price for U.S.-produced grains and refined crude products, doesn't it seem unnecessarily restrictive and downright silly to continue to bar U.S. crude producers from seeking the same benefits? Especially since many, if not all of the original reasons for the domestic crude export ban have disappeared?

And that's precisely what two shale oil producing companies and their CEOs have been saying and lobbying for. Along with Sheffield, Harold Hamm, the billionaire CEO of Continental Resources (CLR, one of the largest independents in the Bakken) have been agitating for several years for an end to the export ban.

And in the summer of 2014, through the unilateral decision of the Commerce Department, they sort of got their wish—not through a true end to the export ban, which would require an act of Congress, but instead through a reclassification of oil 'condensates' as a refined product. Before I discuss why this happened and the end results of this limited workaround that could help end the 40-year-old export ban, let's backtrack a moment: is there any reason to retain the 1970s domestic crude oil export ban in 2014?

It turns out there are some very good ones indeed, especially if you're a proponent of astute long-term energy planning and equally concerned about climate change and the fossil fuel industry's connection to its rapid acceleration.

Shale Oil Is a Limited Resource

Start with the premise that United States crude oil resources are different from other natural resources in that they are non-renewable. We could make an argument that U.S. corn and wheat can be generated in a virtually endless supply, whereas fossil fuels cannot. There is a limited supply on which to draw, even if that supply at any one time looks fantastically large and impossible to deplete. It was just this attitude towards conventional drilling in the early part of the 20th century that led to the depletion of domestic production going into the 1970s, making the United States reliant on the Middle East for energy and that made the 1973 oil embargo so dreadfully effective for OPEC in the first place.

With the resurgence of oil drilling in West Texas and North Dakota, we've seen a similar disregard for the limited nature of U.S. crude oil. Sure, new technologies have revitalized old oil areas we thought were spent. But enthusiasm for the potential that these new technologies unleash shouldn't blind anyone to the inevitable decline that these resources will experience. The only question is how soon it will happen.

On this point, there are several differing opinions. The most quoted estimates of recoverable reserves come from the EIA, one of whose very optimistic charts on shale oil can be seen in Figure 1-2 in Chapter 1 on Saudi America. While looking at this chart, understand this: whatever optimism might be in the figures of the EIA are to the direct benefit of oil companies; their future profits and stock valuations are based on how much oil they can potentially produce now and in the future. Not to be too cynical about it, but at the very least, if the EIA continues to make very enthusiastic guesses on how much oil is really out there, it certainly isn't to the benefit of the oil industry to try and prove the EIA wrong.

Unfortunately, however, the EIA has been consistently wrong. In the Marcellus shale formation (the largest potential reserve of natural gas located through Pennsylvania, West Virginia, and New York State), the EIA initially predicted a total recoverable 410 trillion cubic feet of natural gas, which it later revised down 79% to 84 trillion cubic feet. In estimates of recoverable gas in Poland (yes, Poland in Eastern Europe), revisions dropped 99% from an initial estimate of 187 trillion cubic feet to less than 2. In the Monterey shale play in California, an initial estimate of 15.4 billion barrels of recoverable shale oil was revised in early 2014 to 600 million—that's a 98% reduction.

These and other benchmark missteps from the EIA have been precisely pointed out in a report by David Hughes, a geoscientist with 32 years of experience, in the Geological Survey of Canada called "Drilling Deeper." His findings for the EIA's future predictions on the amount of recoverable shale oil are as disturbing as the already bad history the EIA has shown. In his report, Mr. Hughes believes the decline rates for shale oil wells (that is, how fast they become empty and which we've discussed a bit in comparing shale to a Ponzi scheme,) is much quicker than the EIA predicts overall. Therefore, much of what can be recovered is 'front-loaded.' He predicts a much lower total cumulative production from the Bakken and Eagle Ford shales (which are the two largest U.S. plays), and he further predicts that they will be virtually emptied long before 2040.

But perhaps the most disturbing opinion Mr. Hughes has that differs from the EIA is in the future potential of other remaining shale plays outside of these two that are highlighted by the EIA, as shown in Figure 4-4:

Figure 4-4:
Total Oil Needed to Meet EIA Predictions

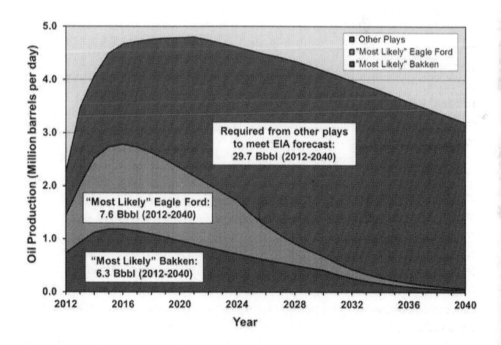

Even with the full-throttle production now taking place in the Bakken and Eagle Ford shale plays, the EIA is confidently relying on production from other plays in the U.S. to make up an almost 30 billion barrel shortfall until 2040 in order to meet its estimates. Even intuitively, this seems more than optimism; it seems like fantasy. Clearly, the Eagle Ford and Bakken represent the 'best of the best' in shale potential or nearly so, and where the EIA expects the next four 'Bakkens' to come from is unclear. But they somehow do expect it.

But no one else does. Even outgoing EOG Resources CEO Mark Papa remarked in 2014 on the U.S. shale boom (in which he had played such an integral part) that all of the 'good' plays and acreage had already been found. He further predicted that no new boom areas even close to the potential of the Bakken or Eagle Ford are all that likely to emerge in the future.

Whether you accept the EIA's numbers or are more inclined to lean towards the findings of Mr. Hughes (as I am), the main point should be clear: U.S. shale resources are not unlimited. When production is booming as it is today, it may seem like shale is infinite, but that is a dangerous myopia that hinders the correct planning for this one-time energy bonanza.

To be clear, I believe we are working with a resource that is likely to be much more limited than most people think. And we have an oil industry that wants to find overseas markets in the midst of a production boom, through an end of the export ban, merely in order to increase profits. But in limiting the oil companies in their access to those markets through a perhaps outdated export ban, some very positive things happen for the United States:

- First, limiting U.S. shale oil to U.S. markets almost certainly slows the speed of production. Even if we're flying along at breakneck speed now, additional access to overseas markets would almost certainly accelerate it further.

- Second, by keeping U.S. oil inside U.S. borders, we enhance our energy independence, supposedly the key goal of shale production. Limiting U.S. crude for the exclusive use of U.S. refineries keeps American oil here in America. There will almost certainly come a time when we again will appreciate the benefits of controlling a domestic energy source for our own use, as opposed to seeing much of it sail off to foreign shores.

- Third, there is an economic benefit that lets the dollars used in procuring energy here in the United States continue to circulate exclusively through the U.S. economy, in refining, storage, and transport.

Should we just allow U.S. oil companies to unilaterally decide when and how quickly to empty our shale resources, when those exports only help other economies grow while growing the wallets of only a handful of oil and gas executives and shareholders? I don't believe now is the time to give a green light to the complete end of the U.S. oil export ban. Despite being an out-of-date directive from a moment long since passed, I believe it still helps prevent an all-out drilling spree in our richest remaining oil fields. And that's a very good thing.

While the U.S. export ban is helping to control the already frantic pace of drilling for shale oil, even to the consternation of many oil companies, it alone could not do enough to prevent the most unexpected and undesirable event shale oil companies could have imagined—a total collapse in the price of crude. Yet we saw such a collapse starting in the late summer of 2014 and extending into the spring of 2015. Understanding how and why that happened is crucial to understanding the future of U.S. shale resources—and the future of U.S. energy. Chapter 5 begins a discussion of this amazing turnaround in prices.

Chapter 5:

THE COLLAPSE OF 2014 OIL

In early October 2014, I got up at 4:30AM to ready myself for a 6AM spot on CNBC to discuss dropping oil prices. With bleary eyes and a long position in both oil and some select oil stocks, I had already taken a helluva beating of losses in both, as oil had slipped towards $75 a barrel from $104 in June. I would finally be forced to liquidate my oil position on Thanksgiving morning when the oil price absolutely cratered after the November OPEC meeting in Vienna delivered no production cut, and that liquidation was after I was greeted that morning with a margin call from my futures broker. Happy Holidays.

But on that October day, I was still convinced that oil's drop was mostly a financial fluke, of two sorts. One was the runaway dollar, which caused a haphazard trade arbitrage in the oil futures. The other was the rather weak appetite of hedge funds and other speculators recently in all hard assets, including copper, gold, and grains, but mostly crude oil. I fully expected both of these financial 'flukes' would clear in the next few days or at most weeks, as traders came back from the Hamptons and realized just how cheap oil was becoming. So I went on the show ready to defend my bullish stance on oil and my belief that this downturn in prices was temporary.

I was met by a foaming Joe Kernan, one of the hosts on the morning Squawk Box show, who didn't even wait for the segment to begin before he started roasting me on air. "The oil market just doesn't want to go the way Dicker says it should!" he announced, teasing the segment (and me) right before a commercial. During the seven-minute segment itself, I was absolutely savaged by Kernan, who took the opportunity to look smart at my expense. The oil market was in freefall and dropping fast: that was the obvious point. But for me, that morning initiated a deeper introspection, because I wasn't yet willing to believe that the rug had been entirely pulled out of the oil market and how I had understood it for the past 10 years.

On the way home from the studio, still driving in the dark and stung, I was too angry to admit more than the fact that, of course, I had gotten the market wrong. It would take a few more weeks before I appreciated how completely the oil market was transforming.

Not seeing that oil was going to lose 50% of its value in late 2014 isn't the worst offence I might have committed; after all, there wasn't a trade house, hedge fund, investment bank analyst, or market pundit who *did* see it coming (except perhaps *Barron's*, which made the prediction in March—5 months before the start of the collapse). Indeed, the final lows for the oil drop might be yet to be seen as I write these lines, and just about every investment bank and trade house analyst has called a few bottoms incorrectly already. Instead, the worst offense I might have committed was to stubbornly deny all the negative inputs that had hit the oil price at once and then further refusing to figure out how they would impact oil in the future. Only with a firm understanding of what had happened and why could I be useful again in analyzing and predicting the best way to trade and invest in oil and energy shares.

There was truly a perfect storm of forces that combined to crater the oil market in late 2014 and change the dynamics of oil exploration and production, particularly shale oil production for perhaps years into the future. Understanding those forces and describing them also proves how silly it is to continue to pursue the myth of U.S. energy independence from oil shale.

The most important and indisputable fact that emerged from the oil crash of 2014 is that shale oil, and the dream of Saudi America, just doesn't work at oil prices below $70 a barrel. Moreover, if lower and less-speculatively-inspired prices for oil are now more likely to become the norm, we've got to entirely rethink our vision of an energy-independent United States.

So what went into the sudden, unexpected, and complete collapse of oil prices in the 2nd half of 2014, and how likely are they to reverse? And what does this 'new oil market' mean for the future of U.S. oil independence?

As usual, the mass media's thoughts on oil's 'demise' have been facile and incomplete. It is never (or almost never) correct to see a big event through the lens of only one or even two changing conditions, and the 2014 oil crash had five huge distortions that I saw converge at once. We need to understand each of them before concluding how the 'new oil market' will impact shale production in the future and the viability of "Saudi America." In no order of importance, I see the top five reasons for the collapse of oil prices in 2014 as:

1. The rise of the U.S. dollar.

2. The defensive market share posture of Saudi Arabia inside OPEC.

3. The increasing production in U.S. shale and the resultant 'oil glut.'

4. The continuing malaise of China and European economies.

5. The demise of U.S. investment banks' commitment to oil marketing—the hiatus of the "endless bid."

Let's take a look at each of these in more depth.

1) Oil and the Rise of the U.S. Dollar

I spent an entire chapter in my first book, *Oil's Endless Bid*, trying to destroy the connection of oil prices to the value of the dollar, so I won't repeat much of that argument here. However, on the face of it, it is so entirely obvious a connection that I have been met with mostly rolling of eyes and scowls when I trot out my arguments against it. Since oil barrels are priced on world markets using the U.S. dollar alone, isn't it patently obvious that a rise in the price of the dollar would translate into a lower price for crude?

Well, it might…and it might not. The U.S. stock market is also priced globally using the U.S. dollar, but a concurrent rise in the 2nd half of 2014 in U.S. equities proved that at least stocks weren't held back by a soaring greenback. The Dow Jones Industrial Average has just settled above 18,000 for the first time ever in December 2014. For some reason, the argument for U.S. stocks as a storehouse of value precisely because they are priced in dollars doesn't equally apply when that storehouse is in a commodity like oil. Why is that? I have no bloody idea. But what is *entirely* true for our purposes is that the relationship *exists*: there is an inverse trade correlation between the price of the dollar and the price of crude oil, as shown in Figure 5-1.

Figure 5-1:
Dollar Goes UP, Oil Goes DOWN

In Figure 5-1, we can easily see that during the last half of 2014, there was a measurable and undeniable correlation between the dollar and oil—even if I don't believe it's a logical one. But let's also try to find out to what degree the rise in the dollar had on the cratering price of crude oil.

Let's start with a simple arithmetic model: if we believe in a pure mathematical correlation, we should find a perfect inverse in pricing between the two. For example, if the dollar rose enough to be worth twice what it previously was, and with all other factors being equal, we would expect to be able to buy twice as much oil with our dollars, right? Purchasing power should roughly equate, so a 10% rise in the dollar should translate into a 10% 'discount' on the price of the crude barrel. But at the highs of oil in June of 2014, the dollar index stood at roughly 80, and by the end of the year, it reached about 90. This 12% rise in the dollar equated to a roughly 47% drop in the price of crude. Clearly, something else is going on.

What I posited in my first book was that the dollar and crude don't have a very strong *practical* relationship at all but instead have cemented a positively arc-welded *trade* relationship: there are literally thousands of algorithms being used in automated systems that trade the inverse relationship of the price of the U.S. dollar and crude oil. When that trade is 'working," virtually every machine will recognize that connection and use it to advantage. Quite simply, if you can get enough people (or machines) to believe a relationship is airtight, it will become a self-fulfilling cyber-prophecy. This clearly happened in the late summer and fall of 2014: every move in the dollar was met with an instantaneous and opposite reaction in the price of crude. I would note that the machines are equally adept at sloughing these trades when the relationship is less connected, as happened in 2005, when both the dollar and the price of oil rallied mightily. But for this 6-month period in 2014, you could set your watch by the connected movement of both. During the critical months when oil collapsed, that relationship was as solidly connected as I've ever seen it—and it added tremendous pressure to oil's price.

2) OPEC and Saudi Arabia

One of the most common sound bites heard to describe the fall of oil in 2014 was a conspiracy theory involving Saudi Arabia and OPEC to destroy U.S. shale producers: number two in our "perfect storm" causing the bust. The Saudis had several good reasons to want to see oil prices fall in 2014 (both for their own sake as well as for the future of the OPEC cartel), yet to say that the Saudis were capable of single-handedly destroying the oil markets is to give them far too much credit.

First, let's examine why the Saudis might want to see a price collapse. The foreign policy relationship between the United States and Saudi Arabia had already grown quite thorny by the late summer of 2014. Two particularly difficult State Department initiatives had helped to inflame relations between the number one OPEC producer of oil and the U.S.: the initiation of negotiations with Iran over its nuclear program and the increasing pressure on Israel to craft a negotiated solution with the Palestinians in the West Bank and Gaza.

Saudi Arabia has had and continues to have an uneasy pact with Iran both inside the OPEC cartel and outside of it. Iran, the most prominent Shiite regime in the region, continues to vie for political and economic dominance with the Sunni Saudis in the Middle East. Inside OPEC, policy has continued to be set by the more productive and more influential Saudis for decades, as the Iranians have worked to gain further influence by other means in the region. One clear result of the Iraq war and the fall of Saddam Hussein has been the increasing influence of the Iranians in the Shiite-controlled governments of the newly constituted Iraq. This has been of grave concern to the Saudis, who certainly much preferred a tyrannical Sunni leader holding the Iraqi nation together by force and terror (even one who had threatened invasion in 1990) to a destabilized Iraqi nation dominated by the majority Shiites and their Shiite nation to the East. Iraq, with its potential of 6 million barrels a day or more of production, continues to be a major threat to the Saudi control of OPEC.

But nothing seemed to frighten the Saudis as much as the continuing push and progress towards an Iranian nuclear weapon. Nothing has been as constant a theme in the Middle East as the continuing bloody struggles between Shia and Sunni, both among tribal areas and sovereign nations. And nothing could destabilize a delicate military balance between Shiite and Sunni as a unilaterally held nuclear weapon in the hands of one of them. In the progress towards that aim, Israel has been the most vocal in expressing its concern of a nuclear-armed Iran, but it is only slightly less a concern for the Saudis: King Abdullah reportedly told U.S. negotiator Dennis Ross in 2011 that an Iranian nuclear capability would have to be countered by an equal Saudi capability.

The one Saudi stopgap to a nuclear-armed Iran has been the United States, which has not only expressed its will in preventing Iran from obtaining nuclear weapons, but has continued to apply economic sanctions as punishment for the continued intransigence of Iran towards signed U.N. nuclear development guidelines and facilities inspections.

Both of these assurances began to crack in 2014 as Secretary of State John Kerry initiated negotiations—along with Russia, France, Germany, China, and the U.K.—with the Iranians on nuclear development pathways, while simultaneously loosening sanctions. Although they didn't show it publicly, the Saudis have made very clear their horror at both of these decisions by the United States. Saudi Arabia warned the U.S. not only about the disingenuous negotiating tactics of the Iranians, but of the difficulty in again closing down the economic spigot to the Iranian economy through sanctions, once that spigot was even slightly reopened. In both suggestions from their major Muslim ally in the region, they were ignored. Moreover, the coziness of Iran to the U.S. took on an even more bizarre turn as the Americans began their assault on Islamic State (ISIS) terrorists in the Iraqi north, with intelligence between Iran and the U.S. being swapped for the first time since the Iranian Revolution. A personal visit in March 2014 from President Obama to Saudi Arabia did little to ease Saudi minds. Finally, Saudi airstrikes began in Yemen in March 2015 to directly combat Iran-sponsored Houthi militants. Further Shiite influence in the region seemed to be growing as well in Egypt, where only a military coup in July of 2013 removed the Islamic Brotherhood from power as well as the strong armed resistance of Hamas to Israel in the Summer of 2014.

These changing geopolitical realities have clearly spooked the Saudis, perhaps to the degree that they felt the need to use the one weapon at their disposal—oil prices—to defend the balance of political and economic power in the region. To be sure, lower oil prices damage the Saudi economy. But they much more viciously harm Iran, which is almost entirely dependent on oil revenue to support an already sanction-weakened economy. Saudi Arabia, with the lowest cost per barrel of production anywhere and a state coffer filled to the brim with surplus capital, has a capability to withstand sustained low oil prices for longer than just about anyone else, particularly its natural rival, Iran. Merely as a method to slow the influence of Iran and other Iran-sponsored Shiite groups in the Middle East, it can be argued that the drop in oil prices was greeted with some glee and relief in Riyadh. But there is even more for the Saudis to celebrate.

There was another, perhaps even clearer purpose for Saudi Arabia and OPEC to foster lower oil prices: to help curtail the growing competition from unconventional oil production in Canada and Brazil, but particularly from horizontal drilling of shale in the United States. This book outlines the revolution of horizontal drilling and its impacts, but in this context the new 5 million barrels a day of domestic production brought online since 2010 did much to limit the market share of OPEC barrels into the United States. With production costs in the U.S. nearly 10 times that of most OPEC members, the Saudis know that a sustained low price for crude would go a long way to reestablishing at least some of that market share.

For the Saudis and OPEC, there were plenty of reasons to want to see oil prices collapse in the summer of 2014.

But all that said, there were several indications that the Saudis did not have an outright scheme to crater oil, but instead were coerced by events to stand by and watch as markets imploded. As oil began its decline in the late summer and early fall, much focus was turned on the annual OPEC meeting scheduled to take place in Vienna on Thanksgiving Day in November 2014. Imploding prices were already being traced directly to OPEC, somehow ignoring all the other inputs to falling prices, but moreover putting the responsibility of stabilizing markets on the backs of the annual meeting and a cartel-wide cut in production. With 40% of global supply coming from the members of the cartel, it was a simple calculus: a drop in production targets from OPEC would not only halt the drop in prices, but would, in fact, begin to allow a recovery.

And despite rumors to the contrary, there were steady indications that Saudi Arabia would be more than willing to be part of a production cut at that meeting. Saudi billionaire and sometime advisor to the Saudi throne, Prince Alwaleed bin Talal, assured the public in October 2014 that low oil prices were as harmful to Saudi Arabia as the rest of the cartel members and that the Saudis were not engaging in a price war. Calls for a production cut were most vocally heard inside the cartel from Iraq and Venezuela as the Saudi oil minister, Ali Al-Naimi, made special trips to both Venezuela and Mexico in the week leading up to the OPEC meeting, even attending a joint meeting with Igor Sechin, the head of the Russian oil behemoth Rosneft. One need not speculate very strongly about the nature of these talks. It is certain that the Saudis explained their unique ability to withstand a drop in price for longer than their cartel and non-cartel partners, and they most likely attempted to negotiate a deal on a multilateral production cut. The public Russian reaction from Sechin and Russian oil minister Alexander Novak tells you all you need to know about the likely responses from all who Al-Naimi visited: "Supply is exceeding demand but not critically and it can't lower oil prices in the long term," Sechin said. Even oil prices below $60 "[aren't] so dramatic for us that it would require an immediate supply cut." Novak complained about the request for a unified approach to production from Saudi Arabia: "We are not Saudi Arabia, which has the ability to reduce production quickly, ramp up quickly." Novak concluded by saying, "The price today of about $80 a barrel wasn't described by any of the meeting's participants as so critical that it needs urgent intervention."

One easy assessment of these meetings and statements leading up to the critical OPEC sit-down in Vienna was the unwillingness of any partners, both inside and outside the cartel, of being part of a multilateral production cut. With a greater economic burden and higher breakeven prices for Iran, Venezuela, and Russia, it was clear that they all expected the Saudis to bear the vast majority—if not the entirety—of the production cut.

This the Saudis did not need nor were compelled to do. The meeting in November 2014 was short and expected: no production cut was agreed on, and crude oil dropped $6 dollars on that Thanksgiving Day alone.

3) Overproduction of U.S. Shale Oil

This book is describing the boom and now bust of shale oil production here in the U.S., but in the late summer of 2014, it seemed that the massive success of shale drilling came as a complete surprise to the market. It did not. Oil analysts like to talk about the million-and-a-half-barrel-a-day surplus that caused the oil bust in 2014, as if that glut emerged just as the markets collapsed, but it did not. In fact, the trajectory of oil production from shale here in the U.S. had been well known for at least a year leading up to the drop in prices. And yet a systemic overproduction of oil did not seem to matter much for prices in 2013 and most of 2014.

Although it is impossible to discount the enormous rise of production as a factor in the collapse of oil prices in late 2014, it should be understood that its effect was only clearly felt when these other inputs that I speak of changed as well. A systemic glut in domestic supply that had existed for close to a year did not stop prices from rallying for most of the spring of 2014.

I make this point for one very important reason: just as oversupply has had a 'lagged' effect on market prices, we should equally not expect a shortage of supply (which I very much believe is likely to be the next big market condition) to immediately and single-handedly force prices to rise. It is the curse and conundrum of oil markets to be able to ignore basic economic forces (at least for a long while) while merrily spinning along out of control. One merely needs to look at the spike of oil prices in 2007 when supply was well in hand to be convinced of that. The next few years of a sluggish oil market will prove the same, I believe, on the down side.

4) China and European Slowdowns

It's not particularly useful for an oil expert to begin a very long section on the disappointments surrounding the European and Chinese recoveries from the collapse of the financial markets since 2008, but those disappointments were particularly sharp in the summer of 2014. In Europe, the difficulties in European Union member states like Greece, Italy, Spain, and Portugal with massive unemployment and possible sovereign debt default continued to plague any real recovery, and the European Union as a whole has continued to suffer through negative GDP growth through 2012 and 2013. But in 2014, the 'showdown' between the strict austerity champions in Germany seemed to come to a head against the more relaxed monetary policies finally advocated by the European Central Bank (ECB). Ultimately, the ECB would gain some room to initiate a bond-buying program similar to that employed by the U.S. Federal Reserve, and the threats of EU exit by Greece would fade, but during the summer of 2014, this was hardly sure.

Worse were the numbers of missed target growth out of China, represented in PMI reports and increasing stockpiles of commodities, particularly copper and oil. Again, an oil expert is hardly the person to get definitive analysis concerning the disappointments of the Chinese economy compared to the official projections that were being proffered, but it was clear to even the eyes of this oil trader that Chinese numbers were being more closely watched and government predictions of GDP growth were being treated in 2014 with more suspicion than ever—and rightly so.

5) The Demise of the U.S. Investment Bank Oil Business

Number five introduces the first really new insight I can deliver into the collapse of oil prices in 2014. Moreover, if you are predicting where oil prices will go in the next several years, I believe this reason is also the most important. It is this mega-change in the pricing of oil that will ultimately decide the long-term viability of shale oil production here in the U.S. and a vibrant, independent United States energy market that allows the dream of Saudi America to come true—or instead to crash and burn.

I've always viewed oil and oil prices with a different perspective than most analysts, who like to assess the *fundamentals* of oil production and demand before turning to the markets and their reaction to those fundamentals. In contrast, I've always found it more important to analyze the *dynamics* that go into the pricing of oil, before turning to the oil fundamentals and seeing where they agree (or don't). At its most simple level, the price of oil is set by buyers and sellers. On any day, if there are more buyers than sellers, you'll see prices rise. Find more sellers, and they'll have to search at lower prices to coerce buyers to come in. It's simple: a market's collective appetite to buy or sell is the only and ultimate price setter. Each buyer and seller *could* have a fundamental reason for approaching a market, and we almost always associate their motivations with a fundamental reason, but nothing says they *need* to have one.

For example, imagine I am your local heating oil distributor and I want to be able to offer a set price to my customers for the coming winter. I can do that by using the futures market to protect myself from rising prices later in the season. Or I could be a small producer in East Texas looking to hedge my production and guarantee my profits well before the oil has even been drilled. But in the modern financial markets, the majority of buyers and sellers are not commercial players like these with easily recognizable fundamental purposes, but passive and active investors and traders both buying and selling financial oil as either an investment or as a speculative trade. And although we would expect that the fundamentals of supply and demand in the physical oil world would impact these players as well, it should also be clear that it doesn't have to impact them much—or at all. If I am a hedge fund that trades oil against oil stocks, I don't care a whit about global supply; instead, my concern is the relative price of Chevron or Hess shares. If I am an individual investor concerned about inflation, I might be a buyer of oil if only because interest rates are rising and nothing more. For the vast majority of players betting on the price of oil, I'm going to be a buyer or a seller if, and only if, I think the price is going higher or lower—and I won't give one damn about the fundamentals. If watching the movement of the dollar is working, great. If bond markets are giving me an insight, terrific. If reading Chinese fortune cookie numbers at lunch shows a correlation, as long as it makes money, fantastic. It is this kind of player who has dominated oil trade since the turn of the millennium.

So, more buyers than sellers will drive market prices higher; and if one group outsizes the other for months or years, we'll see a long-term trend form of consistently higher prices. My thesis in my book *Oil's Endless Bid* was based precisely on that idea: that the number of buyers—indeed, mostly speculative buyers—was in fact consistently outsizing the number of sellers for years leading up to the rapid crash of prices in 2007. Some of these buyers accessed the markets with new futures products, passive indexes, and ETFs, but many of the larger new ones were strongly inspired by the marketing departments of the large U.S. investment banks, who were feeding their own, vastly profitable, proprietary trading desks.

But since early 2014, the rapid sale by investment banks of their physical assets and proprietary trading oil desks (and their associated marketing arms) has removed a source of many of the buyers. And what might be 'worse," at least for the future of U.S. oil independence, is that that 'inspiration' to buy oil is not likely to reemerge any time soon.

On Friday, November 14, 2014, I did a segment with Chris Hayes on his MSNBC show, explaining how the fall of proprietary trading inside the investment banks meant the end of the speculative 'pillow' of money that had buoyed oil prices for years. He immediately got it:

"When oil prices were high, you were one of the few who pointed out that it was 'hot money' flowing into the markets that was causing it, and everyone around said you were crazy—a lefty idiot. Now, with a lot of those places closing their desks, there's less money in the trade, and prices are coming down."

Indeed. Truly a simplification, made necessary by television, but it's dead on the money. I've gone through a number of other, more measurable reasons for oil's collapse in 2014. But really, are any of them sufficient to explain a 50% drop in less than 6 months' time? Even in combination, a drop like this in the price of the most important commodity in the world would indicate a massive economic displacement—a credit crisis somewhere or a global depression like we saw in 2008—and we're seeing nothing like that (or at least we hope not). Only the rapid retreat of the 'bid' in oil from those who have slavishly bid for oil since 2010 could make such a disaster occur. And it is the investment banks that had delivered that bid through their trading and marketing departments before their dispersal from the industry throughout 2014.

In March of 2014, J.P. Morgan entered into an agreement to sell its commodity unit along with several physical assets to Mercuria, a private trading group started by two ex-Goldman Sachs traders, for a reported $3.5 billion. Not surprisingly, the deal closed in October 2014. In April 2014, Barclays announced that it was shopping its physical assets in commodities and also looking for an appropriate buyer of its trading group, but Barclays did not wait to find one before beginning to scale back on its commodity operations and start letting traders go. Back in December 2013, Deutsche Bank didn't even bother looking for a buyer; it just shut down its oil desk and let go of its 200 employees in the division. Also in December 2013, Morgan Stanley—the largest physical broker of oil and oil derivatives on Wall Street—fully cut the cord with its oil pipeline and storage business with Transmontaigne and then entered into an agreement to sell the rest of the assets and the trading operations in total to Russian oil behemoth Rosneft for an undisclosed sum. However, by the end of 2014, the Russians were balking at the sale, and it ultimately didn't close because of sliding oil prices. But the damage was already done: Morgan Stanley was left with a husk of its former preeminent trading unit and was again looking for a buyer.

The reasons for the sales are clear and come because of two reasons: First, the entire client/trade relationship of the major oil desks was shattered by the financial crisis and the fall of oil in 2008. It must be remembered that the banks themselves were in some of the deepest distress as a result of the financial crisis. Bad derivatives and the need for bailouts forced not only major internal disruptions and restructurings inside the banks, but also a very apparent 'self-regard' became readily obvious inside the trading departments. To be blunt, the major investment banks were looking to save themselves first and put many of their clients' needs on the bottom of their lists. As a consequence, many of the relationships that bank marketing departments had built over years were destroyed. New leaders installed into old desks as a result of the many restructurings inside the commodity divisions did not inspire new clients to begin to trade, nor did it inspire old clients to remain loyal or even continue to buy into marketing pitches for 'hedges' and hard-asset diversification.

Perhaps even more important is the second reason: if those client relationships showing stress weren't enough to shatter bank business, Dodd-Frank and the Volcker rule did the rest. Heavy new capitalization requirements, along with new requirements on clearing and trade reportage, made many of the 'old school' oil trades that supported the bank desks much more expensive and more scrutinized by the CFTC and other regulatory agencies than ever. The kitchen just became too hot, and the heat has driven the major banks out of many portions of the commodity game.

And as I talked about extensively in *Oil's Endless Bid*, investment bank institutional clients were overwhelmingly and singularly buyers of oil and other commodities. On the other end of investment bank trading desks were the oil companies themselves, always available to 'sell': you can say that oil companies are always 'long' oil and will be approaching the oil markets with sell offers of products they produce. It was the job of the marketing departments inside the big banks to help bring in the buyers needed to offset those natural sellers and make a market through which the bank traders could sit in the middle and profitably trade. This they did only too well: I posited that much of the premium in the oil market we saw through 2007 was due to the overwhelming success of developing interested buyers of oil. But finally in 2014, with the sale, slowdown and often shutdown of many of the investment bank desks (although Goldman Sachs continues to carry on), that shifted.

The new, mostly private players in the oil trade game that replaced the banks—such as Glencore, Vitol, and Mercuria—just didn't have the same model for developing retail clients through marketing (that is, for finding speculators). These privately held companies are focused more towards controlling the physical space in the commodity world than in trying to make their money solely from trading. For example, Glencore is a massive trader of commodities, but its name is known much more widely because of its long-term plan of buying up mining assets; the trade that flows from the ownership of those assets, although very profitable, has become secondary. Goldman Sachs was the target of a Federal probe on its metals storage facilities, and soon after, Goldman sold its aluminum warehousing facilities to Reuben Brothers, a private Swiss firm. Similarly, J.P. Morgan has exited the copper warehousing business. Both of these moves represent sloughing of physical assets from banks that used them as conduits for trading as opposed to profit centers from storage. The complete collapse of the metals markets at the same time as the demise of oil prices is hardly a coincidence: it is a function of the same retreat from the trading business surrounding physical commodity assets by all the major global financial powerhouses—Morgan Stanley, J.P. Morgan, Deutsche Bank, Barclays, and Goldman Sachs. The golden days of commodities, at least for the investment banks, seem to be coming to an end.

When thinking about why I was unable to see the massive collapse of oil prices in 2014, I believe this was my deepest myopia—believing that the bid that I outlined in my book in 2011 was going to turn out to be, for all intents and purposes, "endless." I had assumed that the growth of investment bank interest, trading, marketing, and leverage in financial oil was in its earliest stages and would continue unfettered for decades. Instead, that growth has not only been slowed; in many cases, it has stopped altogether. In my mind and throughout my career, I had seen the investment bank dominance in oil at times outweigh every other factor in the market, whether fundamental and financial. I saw the financial crisis and the subsequent bank 'bailouts' as a mere speed bump in the road for them, and laughed at the Basel II and later Basel III regulatory frameworks. Dodd-Frank and the Volcker rule wasn't going to slow down this group of brilliant, hungry, and savvy financial minds—I was sure of it.

But it has. Oil's endless bid has turned out to be not quite so endless after all. To me, out of all the factors that contributed to oil's collapse, the end of the 'Endless Bid' has been the most overlooked and also the most important.

Oil's price collapse in 2014 has been unique in that it hasn't been accompanied by a concurrent collapse in the U.S. or global economy; in fact, it has come while economies have been (at least sluggishly) recovering. This makes the event worthy of further analysis and worth figuring out the reasons oil has disconnected from other asset classes and how long this bust will last. The next chapter looks to answer those questions.

Chapter 6:

ANALYSIS OF THE 5 REASONS:
WHY THE SHALE BUST WAS SO COMPLETE

If the U.S. wishes to continue to pursue a dream of energy independence, I think I've proven that oil prices need to stay fairly high, and even more important, stable. This was the reason for the deep analysis of the collapse of prices in 2014: if we're destined to see a market that violently swings back and forth between extremes, it will be impossible to count on steadily producing domestic shale resources.

But there's something more important to consider. Everyone in the world of energy in 2014—legislators in Washington, small and large exploration companies, manufacturers of machinery, car makers, pipeline operators, drilling engineers, utility schedulers—every one of them considered high oil prices to be dependable and constant. A $100+ price for a barrel of oil was considered but a starting point, with most expecting steady rises, or at worst (at best?) slight but measurable weakening. Everyone was caught by surprise by the $50 shellacking that oil took in late 2014. Sub-$50 prices for oil changes the calculus for energy everywhere: on energy policy in Washington, development of shale and offshore resources, the Arctic, export of oil and natural gas, Keystone XL and other pipeline projects, auto emissions requirements, and of course the future of renewable fuels development and other climate change initiatives.

Figuring out how all of the previous chapter's inputs coalesced to crater oil prices then becomes critical indeed. Is this drop in prices just another down cycle, like the last one we saw in 2008 or is it unique? What does the way prices dropped tell us about our goals of independence from foreign sources of energy? If we're lucky and we're just working through another market displacement like the last one, perhaps we can still make plans for gaining energy independence and perhaps plan a weaning away from fossil fuels altogether. If, however, this latest mess in oil is something completely different, something unknown, recurrent, and unpredictable, then we'll have more than a small problem charting any steady course in the future.

Unfortunately, this is precisely what I see happening.

This latest 55% collapse in the price of oil is at least reminiscent in speed and surprise to 2008, when the financial appetite for oil as a hard asset (along with much of the credit on which it relied) disappeared—and oil dropped more than 70% in a similarly short amount of time. Let's go back for a moment to that big move up and quick move down and see if there are any parallels. The quadrupling in the price of oil from about $35 a barrel in 2003 through the 2007 spike to above $140 a barrel can be attributed to many fundamental factors, including the rising growth in China and other emerging markets. Turbocharging that move higher was a new wave of financial investment and trading, much of which came from bank trading activity and the sale of innovative derivatives, which allowed virtually anyone to invest in oil. In late 2007, we saw the price of oil fall apart as all of that investment capital that had buoyed prices violently retreated, both from dedicated traders as well as longer-term hedge fund and ETF investors. Markets began recovering slowly again in 2008, as the restoration of credit by the Federal Reserve and bailouts of the major investment banks began to restore confidence in all the derivative markets, and oil began to march once more towards and beyond $100 a barrel.

That is my very thumbnail sketch of oil pricing for the past 10 years. The point is that very large changes in oil prices have usually had very specific and strong financial stimuli, most often caused by financial stress or outright crisis. But this latest collapse of prices starting in the late summer of 2014 seemed to have had few, if any, of these same earmarks. That makes it tougher to figure out what is really going on and why.

Let's come back to the present: the five factors I outlined in Chapter 5 seem collectively to have accounted for oil's big break. So maybe if we can figure out whether and for how long those unique inputs to the markets are around, maybe we can try to predict oil's next move, and perhaps even when it will make it. That should help in our plan for another new renaissance in U.S. oil, and the next shale boom.

Not surprisingly, it might also give us some good ideas for oil patch investment.

Let's take another look at those five factors.

1. Dollar Strength

One thing we can be relatively sure of is that the unprecedented rise of the dollar isn't at all likely to be a 'new normal.' It would be financially deadly for both Europe and the U.S. if the dollar would approach a long-term trade close to parity with the Euro. Even more dangerous would be a constantly weak Ruble where Russian sovereign debt would be at a consistent risk of default. Rather, it is clear that the promise of the end of quantitative easing and an inevitable tightening of monetary policy here in the U.S. in 2015 has been running smack up against a European Union and Japanese economy looking to heavily stimulate growth through monetary policy of their own. That's the scene we're setting today in 2015, but we won't forever see Europe and Japan chase the U.S. dollar to the bottom as we're seeing it happen now. We can be reasonably sure that the dollar won't always be the world's favorite currency.

But how long will it take for that to change? U.S. Federal Reserve Quantitative Easing (QE) programs are 7 years old now, and everyone recognizes the end is coming. In Europe, however, where austerity was the watchword through much of the economic crisis and non-recovery since, they're just getting started. Bond-buying programs that have been the big Fed policy initiative here in the U.S. are just beginning inside the European Central Bank in 2015, with an initial 30 billion Euros announced in late January. That goes almost equally well for Japan. These initiatives will take some serious time, however: first, to take hold in Europe, where there is still more than a little resistance to stimulative spending ideas; and second, to see the real throttling back on interest rates from a U.S. Federal Reserve. In short, although you can't bet that the U.S. dollar will be perennially strong, I wouldn't bet on a sustained turnaround anytime soon—certainly not until mid-2016 at the earliest.

2. Saudi Arabia and OPEC

Inside OPEC are three economies that are very reliant on high oil prices to balance budgets: Iran, Venezuela, and Saudi Arabia, as shown in Figure 6-1.

Figure 6-1:
Balancing the Budget with Oil

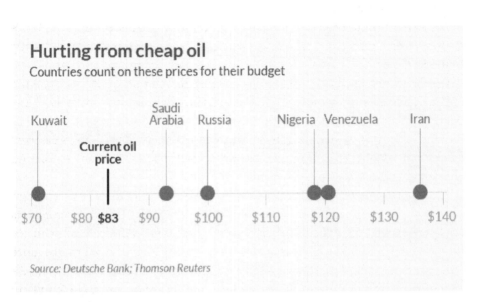

Hurting from cheap oil
Countries count on these prices for their budget

Source: Deutsche Bank; Thomson Reuters

None of these countries, including Saudi Arabia, could possibly be happy about low energy prices. However, the Saudis hold a unique position in the energy world. While they might need $90+ oil to balance their state budget, they need not be solely reliant on current oil revenues to do it, unlike others, like Iran and Venezuela. With sovereign reserves that have had literally decades to load up on U.S. Dollars and with social responsibilities a fraction of other western and oil-rich nations, the Saudis are uniquely capable of withstanding low oil prices for virtually longer than just about anyone. Even with $40 oil, the Saudis make a significant profit on their oil, whose cost of production is less than $10 a barrel, while equivalent costs of production can be 4 to 9 times more expensive for everyone else outside of the Middle East. If the Saudis are intent on playing chicken with other OPEC members, they certainly can do it. More important for our conversation, if the Saudis also want to take the opportunity to squeeze U.S. shale players—by waiting for those marginal producers in the Bakken, Eagle Ford, Permian, and other lesser plays to scream 'Uncle!' and clear out of the way—you can bet every dime you've got that they can continue careening down that track at 70 mph in a two-and-a-half-ton truck, with little regard to what might be blocking the road. U.S. shale producers are facing a very formidable and resilient challenge with a Saudi kingdom prepared to pump any volume of oil and protect its customer base.

As I pointed out in Chapter 5, I am not of the belief that the Saudis contemplated a 'conspiracy' plan to crater prices in 2014 in order to destroy United States shale production. I've pointed out several other reasons why I believe oil began to decline starting in the late summer of 2014, while the critical decision not to cut production inside OPEC did not come until late November of that year. Instead, I think the Saudis took what they saw as a grand opportunity in dropping prices and chose (deliberately, to be sure) to get out of the way, allowing their pass at a production cut to further accelerate the decline.

But having embraced the opportunity and embarked on this strategy, it is impossible to believe that the Saudis will abandon it until it has had its cold, calculated effect. Having made clear their willingness and ability to see oil prices go under $50 a barrel, you can bet that they will need to see more than a few U.S. producers disappear from the supply chain before the Saudis change course. If the global marketplace was suffering from a 1.2 million barrel a day 'surplus' before the drop in prices, I would expect the Saudis will want to see a reduction in U.S. production of about that much before even considering a production cut and easing that price pressure. Until then, you would expect the Saudis to continue their tough strategy of retaining market share, and even increasing it, at any price the market delivers. With the EIA still projecting increasing production in the U.S. through much of 2015, it would be foolish to expect the Saudis to be the source of a recovering crude price for at least a year, if not more.

3. U.S. Shale Production

Of the 5 reasons for oil's collapse, the arrest of U.S. production growth seems the likeliest to adjust the fastest—but it will also be painfully slow. Each and every barrel less that hits the market will be accompanied by the raving, kicking, and screaming of its producer. U.S. exploration and production companies saw their best share price growth during the first stage of the shale boom from one metric alone: increased production growth. Although so many other factors are likely to matter to the long-term viability of any

E+P, even the most haphazardly financed and inefficient oil producer was rewarded through 2014 if it merely showed increasing production in one of the 'hot' shale plays, and damn the costs. To admit to a production decline (or even to plan for one in a new, lower oil environment) is a black mark that no oil company CEO was willing to admit to. Even as I write this in February 2015, Magnum Hunter CEO Gary Evans released a statement saying that he was cutting Capex to zero for the coming year, while claiming he will increase production 100%.

Not all oil company heads are as optimistic as Evans. Nor are the budget slashes as extreme. But the dire nature of the oil collapse has shattered the proposed spending in virtually every U.S. E+P, as shown in Table 6-1.

Table 6-1: U.S. Shale Companies Stop Spending

Company	2015 U.S. Capex	2015 vs. 2014 Capex
Apache	$4 billion	down 26%
Conoco-Phillips	$13.5 billion	down 20%
Continental Resources	$4.6 billion	down 12%
Denbury Resources	$500 million	down 50%
Energy XII	$670 million	down 17%
Goodrich Petroleum	$175 million	down 50%
Halcon Resources	$750 million	down 20%
Oasis Petroleum	$800 million	down 42.8%
Rosetta Resources	$950 million	down 20%
Swift Energy	$250 million	down 36%

Not one of these companies, however, admitted a production slowdown might come as well in 2015 in the wake of these massive drops in spends. In fact, most refused to revise their production projections even one iota in light of the oil collapse. In their very weak defense, admitting less drilling while not admitting less oil isn't an outright lie. There is a distinct lag in the time when money begins on a project and oil is produced. Even in the shale plays, where oil is only 4 to 6 months away from a well site being selected and oil first coming out of the ground, there remains for these companies a producing inventory of projects undertaken when oil prices remained near and above $100 a barrel.

But shale oil's advantages of cheap costs and short delay between drill bit and oil at the wellhead is also its deepest failing because new wells must be constantly found and put into service. Quite frankly, that means that the gargantuan drop in the budgets of U.S. oil companies will necessarily translate into reduced production at some point. Moreover, whenever it shows up, it will be months or even years sooner than for just about any other oil-procurement process.

How soon? That is the question that plagues oil analysts almost as much as it does energy company CEOs. According to the U.S. watchdog EIA, not for a year at least. The EIA projects increasing U.S. production through the end of 2015. But the EIA is almost always wrong, sometimes stunningly so. Even with the most conservative estimate of when slashed budgeting on drilling will actually result in a slowdown of oil hitting the market, you'd not expect anything much of the shale 'boom' trajectory to change even a little at least until the late fall of 2015 and more likely in the early months of 2016.

Without a measurable slowdown in oil production in the U.S., we can't expect the fundamental of supply to have a quick response on oil prices either.

4. China and Europe

Literally on the day that I'm writing this in early 2015, the Chinese have released GDP results for 2014, claiming growth of 7.4%, just missing official targets of 7.5% (see Figure 6-2). I'm not the only one laughing at this ridiculous figure. The markets, first up on the news in the premarket by as much as 10 S&P points is currently down 15. Nobody believes the Chinese on their numbers, and why should they? Literally every other metric on China that's being tracked that isn't mediated by the central government is showing far worse than a 7.4% growth rate. The suspicions of Chinese economic results from the central government have become, if anything, worse than they were in 2014 when the oil bust began.

In Europe, nervousness over Greece has again arisen in 2015. The talk of another possible exit scenario (Grexit) from the European Union over restructuring of debt, followed by other weaker E.U. members leaving as well, has stalled what was a pretty strong start in many of the European stock indexes for 2015. Although many investment analysts still consider Europe to be a strong equity opportunity in 2015, the reappearance of old issues from the financial crisis (which is now close to seven years old) continue to make Europe a difficult bet for resurgent growth.

What does all this mean for oil? Well, as I've said many times, you're not likely to get definitive analysis on China and Europe from an oil trader...but from what I've witnessed, there's little to believe that the economic picture in either place is about to magically clear anytime soon.

No, if oil is getting ready to rally back to $100 a barrel, it won't likely be because of massively increasing demand from China, as in 2003-2007, or from a completely stable and robust European picture either.

5. U.S. Investment Bank Speculative Interest

Nothing has been as fascinating for me to watch as the changes inside the oil markets since the financial crisis. I made my career as an oil trader, and during those years, the big investment banks were the most important players to measure. Their dominance of the oil markets was so important and underappreciated that I wrote my first book, *Oil's Endless Bid*, to describe their influence. My inability to connect their retreat from financial oil to dropping prices in late 2014 was a big reason I didn't see the scale of the shale bust coming. But the changeover in financial dominance is nearly complete now.

I was watching some of the interviews from Davos at the 2015 World Economic Forum, when Jamie Dimon, head of JPMorgan Chase, came on for an interview. While trying furiously not to sound like a complainer, he sounded ever more so as he outlined the vast amounts of extra capital his bank was being forced to sit on under the new regulatory guidelines. Leaders at MetLife and AIG had expressed similar 'concerns.' But this is not a rocket science code that Dimon and others were expressing here; they were bemoaning the inability to do the kind of speculative, proprietary, leveraged businesses that made them mountains of money before 2008, and the markets, with their easy credit and tempting volatility, were beckoning for them to do again. Fixed-income (bond-trading) revenues at all the major banks, normally a proprietary trading goldmine, have become a quarterly disappointment, dropping significantly and regularly.

And then there are the commodities.

In Chapter 5, I outlined the exodus of the investment banks from the commodity and oil sphere beginning in 2014, starting on the physical side of the business and then necessarily moving on to the disbandment of the trading groups. I am a firm believer that, out of the 5 reasons I've isolated for the rapid fall in the price of crude, the departure of investment bank marketing and trade has been certainly the least appreciated and perhaps also the most important. The 'new' owners of the derivative world who have filled the vacuum—including Vitol, Trifigura, Mercuria, and Glencore—are privately owned and not under the same scrutiny, and they are a far different breed of trader than those who used to roam the investment bank desk.

And understandably so: the investment banks were a unique construct of several cross-pollinating businesses under one roof that just led to opportunity after opportunity. There just isn't the kind of cross-product opportunity inside any of these private derivative monsters as there was inside the investment banks. Goldman Sachs and Morgan Stanley, for example, weren't just trading commodities back in the day; they had direct daily contact with clients who were using and producing these commodities. And their relationship with these sellers and buyers went far beyond mere work inside the commodity space. They helped issue and trade corporate bonds for Kellogg's and ADM and Chevron; they worked on the merger opportunity between Halliburton and Baker Hughes; they structured and found investors for the split of Phillips 66 from its parent company Conoco-Phillips; and they prepared the IPO of Athlon Energy and dozens of other start-up oil companies every year. Financial services for major corporate clients extended well beyond mere futures hedging.

On the other side of the building, there were hundreds of account executives helping to invest the pensions of the North Carolina Highway workers and other major pension funds, the endowment at Yale or other major universities, and the accounts of thousands of high-net-worth family trusts. The synergies between those roles and the work inside the commodity trading and marketing desks were magnificently strong, no matter what 'Chinese Walls' are pretended to exist. Business breeds business, and nowhere was that more evident than in the commodity business for the major investment banks.

Neither Vitol, Glencore, nor any of the other private trade houses based in Switzerland have relationships anywhere nearly as good as that. Let's be very clear about what I'm talking about here: the change that I'm outlining is a turnover in the most significant players that are going to dominate financial oil for the next several years. When I wrote about the influence of investment banks into the oil market in 2011, I never ever expected that influence to disintegrate so completely, nor did I expect this next group of traders to so quickly fill the vacuum that was being left behind. But none of these private trading houses have the amazing synergies that JP Morgan and Goldman Sachs presented to the energy markets.

Consequently, when the next bull market condition in oil *does* come along (as it most definitely must), there won't be anyone nearly as good, nearly as connected, or nearly as experienced at selling it to the market— and by that I mean finding the commercial and retail interest in trading and investing in oil.

Those customer-based, proprietary trade business 'golden days' inside the investment banks seem gone forever. For the U.S. investment banks, that was a unique moment in time captured profitably by only a few select integrated financial institutions. But is it never to be repeated again?

I firmly believe that the next fundamental shortage in oil will find a way to be taken advantage of by *someone* in the financial sphere. Will it be the investment banks? It's hard to imagine they could repeat their magic: they'll need to lobby even harder than they already have to get the capitalization requirements laid upon them by Dodd-Frank significantly weakened. Will they also be willing to reconstitute desks that they so recently disbanded and start hiring back traders?

It would be a long row for them to hoe. It's tough to predict the outcome of bank lobbying in Washington to relax capital requirements, but Jamie Dimon and other bank executives seem prepared to continue the fight. And you should expect bank lawyers and lobbyists to make some progress in creating whatever loopholes they need to lessen capital (and reporting) requirements and get back, at least partially, into the commodity game. You can see that already brewing with the newly elected Republican Congress and various changes inside the CFTC and SEC.

And if they get that accomplished, hiring back traders is easy.

But none of that happens quickly. All of it will take time.

My point is not that the banks won't again be a force in rising oil prices when they begin to rise again, because they could try to reconstitute their presence when the time is right. My point is they aren't positioned right now at least to take advantage of a spiking oil market. They will—fortunately or unfortunately, depending on your point of view—be late for this party in a way that they weren't in 2003 and in 2009.

In short, a quick recovery of oil prices is unlikely to come from the investment banks.

Chapter 7:

THREE PHASES TO SHALE BUST

We finally come to the moment where we can try to decipher what the whole shale energy boom has been about. Has it helped the United States to become energy independent? Has it freed us from the bonds of our enemies? Are we economically more stable because of it? Are our people benefitting from lower gas prices and our businesses from lower energy costs? Or has the whole shale boom been more about the freedom to exploit our own domestic resources the only way Americans can, using technical superiority mixed in with the hubris of free-market capitalism?

And what about the shale bust that is now upon us? Now that the shares of so many of the smartest and most innovative oil companies are battling to stave off bankruptcy, find new capital, and restructure, what can we learn? Has the United States been over-confident and over-enthusiastic about the benefits of shale oil and gas? To be sure, the small group of oil entrepreneurs who led us on this road of shale boom and bust have been smart and innovative. But is smart and innovative enough around which to craft a consistent U.S. energy policy?

The oil is there. Not only do we have a really good idea of how much is there, but we also know how to get it out. That should have translated into an incredible, amazing economic advantage for the United States. It could have been the basis for an economy that outpaced on every metric and for an explosion in middle-class jobs and rising wages. Some of that, despite everything, has happened.

But, on balance, what we've done with that largesse, what we've just seen with the indiscriminate drilling and flaring, financing and public offerings, boom and bust cycle from 2009 to today has been a wide-scale disaster. You could count on one hand the number of people who have largely benefitted from the shale boom: a small number of resourceful, shrewd people with incredible initiative to be sure, with names like Hamm and McClendon and Mitchell. For the people who served under them and did the real innovating—the experimentation with drill angles and fracking fluids and cement—the rewards have been far more modest. And for the American public, the rewards have been practically non-existent.

For a resource that is unique to the United States and one that we all must depend on, that hardly seems fair.

So far, I've written this book on shale oil, concentrating almost exclusively on *price*. I think that might have confused many people who began this book looking for a public policy statement or an investment thesis. But I've wanted to explain as best I can the inputs into price, both fundamental and financial, as well as try to explain the mechanism for price motion, both here in the U.S. and globally, for a reason. I'm hoping you'll feel rewarded for your efforts if you've stayed with me thus far. Digesting the many fundamental, financial, and psychological inputs affecting price action is always going to be the biggest hurdle for people trying to really understand energy markets, but it is critical. I continue to study, trade, and write about the energy markets because I continue to be astounded and fascinated by them.

Here's one insight from this 30-year veteran of the energy markets: the oil market is quite frankly nuts in how it prices oil and has been, in my opinion, off the rails since the start of the millennium. We have seen several times in the last 15 years when oil prices extended well beyond what any explanation of supply and demand fundamentals could reasonably give it, no matter what specious explanation was proffered in *The Wall Street Journal* or discussed on Bloomberg TV. 2008 was obviously the most egregious example of this, and the reasons for that lunacy spike in prices above $145 a barrel was the subject of my first book, *Oil's Endless Bid*. But as I write this, oil is now alternatively below any price that fundamentals could reasonably support (it's trading at about $45 a barrel), and at this price, more than 25% of the oil production we currently depend on to keep our planet spinning is suddenly uneconomic and selling at a loss.

Do either of these extremes make any logical sense? No.

But can we understand why these extremes have been reached? Yes. And by understanding, we can build a plan not only for investment, but also, hopefully for public policy.

Price extremes define oil because price means everything. It is paramount. It motivates every move that every oil company makes in the present. Their expectations of price motivate every move they will make in the future. From price, they decide where to search for oil, how much they are willing to pay for the land or sea where they will drill, how long they'll sink money into the project, and how quickly they might abandon the hole they've made.

For those using oil on the other side of the sales counter, it's no different. Oil prices determine the cars and trucks Ford will plan on building. They will determine the average cost United will charge for a seat on a flight to Paris, France and whether the airline will continue to service the smaller municipal airport in Paris, Texas. They'll affect your choice on whether or not to have solar panels installed on your roof and whether you'll take your family vacation heading out to the Grand Canyon in a rented Winnebago or instead stay at home relaxing at the local pool.

And price ultimately dictates public policy as well. It will determine whether subsidies for wind and geothermal energy will continue to be funded and whether incentives will be paid for the purchase of electric cars. It will be the ultimate determinant in whether the Keystone pipeline will be built, and it was clearly the ultimate factor in the "courage" Governor Andrew Cuomo showed in his ban on fracking in New York State. It will also unfortunately determine just how quickly we recognize as a nation the growing dangers posed by climate change and the need to develop an energy economy based on sustainable renewable energy sources.

Price is everything.

And what I know about price—what has been proven to me again and again—is that oil prices have become ever more unreliable as the systems that work on it become ever more financialized. Of all the things I have studied and correctly and incorrectly forecasted in my 30+ years in the oil markets, the one unshakable truth I have held onto is that the wide ranges of prices for oil we have seen in the last 15 years have been tethered far more to unrelated financial inputs than to the underlying fundamentals of oil. It has been those financial "gremlins" inside the machine that have made oil prices go so far above any logical expectation so many times, particularly in 2007 and 2010 and equally foolishly low as in 2009 and in 2015. Those wide extremes in price have done more than make and lose fortunes in the oil world. They've affected just about everything politically and socially in the rest of the world. Maybe someday, someone will write a book about the effects of oil volatility on global politics. It would be a good one.

But for now, let's just try to get a bit more of a handle on price, if it matters so much. I've talked a bit about the shale boom, which was inspired by oil prices that averaged around $100 a barrel from 2010 through 2014, when horizontal drilling and new shale barrels began to come online: see Figure 7-1.

Figure 7-1:
Oil Price Collapse

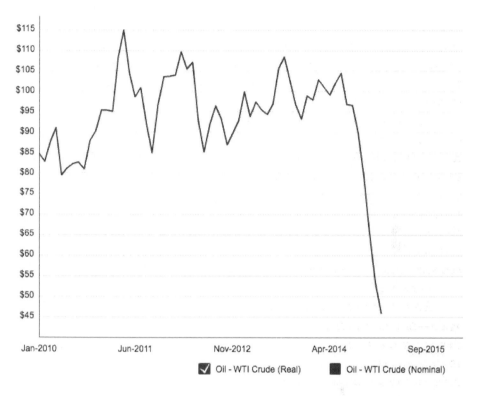

Let's talk about the present oil price bust and how long that might last, as I believe this downturn in prices says far more about the future of energy here in the U.S. than the boom cycle that has preceded it. I've tried to advance the idea that this bust won't be just a "bump in the road" for the oil industry and that all the inputs, both fundamental and financial, that have conspired to drop prices are likely to be with us for a while. But for how long, actually? This is a critical question and matters to the future of U.S. energy. A short dip in prices might not affect U.S. plans much at all. But a very long swoon in prices will necessarily change the landscape of U.S. production completely. I see this shale bust as moving forward in three distinct phases.

Phase I: Living Through the Oil Price Crash

As of early February 2015, we were still in what I would call Phase I of the oil collapse. It's what could be called the 'bail the lifeboats' phase, as virtually every oil producer and oil services company begins a panicked attempt to staunch the hemorrhage of crashing prices and reduced activity. Mostly, this has resulted in a radical cut in spending budgets, as I outlined a bit in Chapter 6. Oil services companies have responded in an equally panicked way by slashing the prices of drilling services they provide as well as by cutting their own spending, trying furiously to cost compete in what they now know will be a shrinking market.

Cutting budgets or slashing prices to customers are actually the easiest things that oil companies and services firms can do. For producers, cutting spending doesn't affect the bottom line immediately, as reductions in capital expenditures (capex) won't result in production declines—and therefore profits—for months in the future. You can even claim continuing high production results despite major drops in capital expenditures, a counter-intuitive result but still at least immediately genuine. Almost all of the independent oil companies have done precisely this through their reporting up to the 4th quarter of 2014, reporting slashed spending yet increasing production forecasts. In fact, at least for the first 6 months after cutting capex, oil company executives can look like stars, chopping off the top line with little immediate effect on the bottom. Further, the projections on capital expenditures are a bit of an accountant's dodge in that they can be adjusted several times over the year to adapt to changing market conditions. An oil company can talk about an extreme cut in spends at the start of the year, but should oil prices allow, it can still ramp spending back up later. Looking responsible using the accountant's pen is a pretty easy way to initially react to a low price environment, and just about everyone is doing it.

When it comes to paring capex, the industry seems to have moved in two very distinct directions: those companies that believe that oil's distress will be relatively short-lived (i.e., perhaps less than 6 months' time) and those that aren't yet sure. Only the better-capitalized players in the shale world have the luxury of taking a chance on a strategy of a short-lived downturn. For those independent oil players that have less than stellar debt positions and shaky cash flows, their strategy is simple: cut spending to the bone and pray. Either crude prices will recover before cash flow and short hedges run out, or they won't; it's all up to the markets now. But for the large-cap shale players with a bit more breathing room and a range of choices they could make for 2015 and 2016, there is still quite a bit of collective hallucination going on.

For example, take Hess: for two years leading up to crude collapse, Hess took on a bold restructuring effort, clearly burning jealously at the fantastic stock gains by some of the independent players in the Bakken, where Hess was one of the very first to invest heavily, gaining a first stake as early as 1981. Since 2012, Hess sold off the entirety of its refining and storage business and what was left of its retail gasoline stations, some of which had been around for more than 50 years. Hess also put its trading business, Hetco, on the market (ultimately sold to a hedge fund!) and doubled down on production, pouring money exclusively into its prime areas in the Gulf of Mexico and the Bakken and Utica shales. The company's bold moves were lauded and rewarded on Wall Street, where shares exploded from $42 in the spring of 2012 to trade over $100 in the summer of 2014.

However, with the downturn in oil, Hess was stuck (as were several others) with their new strategy of production specialization—they looked far less like a 'mini-major' with assets all along the petroleum chain, and more like an independent E+P producer. Hess planned a modest 16% reduction in spending—a small cut for a dedicated shale player. Moreover, Hess vowed to continue to raise production in the Bakken shale, despite owning advantageous leases that, unlike most other Bakken players, did not require immediate drilling. In addition, Hess reaffirmed a share-buyback program that it had planned earlier. This is a strategy that is more appropriate for Hess circa 2010, before it began its bid to focus on liquids production. It also implies a defiant belief that crude oil prices cannot sustain their levels below $65 for more than six months—a hopeful assessment.

Another hallucinating independent, Continental Resources, the largest producer in the Bakken, made the very controversial move of buying back all of its short hedges as prices dropped below $83. Harold Hamm, the company's billionaire CEO who decided on the move, then watched prices move $40 lower still. Mr. Hamm was correct in believing that oil is not fundamentally sustainable below $70 and therefore was convinced that it would surely see a quick rise again, forgetting about the ability of financial markets to often defy logic. When asked about the wisdom of this move, Hamm commented that the "jury was still out" on the trade, despite literally billions of dollars of missed profits. Hamm has proven himself in the past to be an admittedly brilliant oil man, but is not as brilliant an oil trader.

This collective hallucination on the quick recovery of crude prices permeates the industry. As Figure 7-2 shows, there are only a handful of companies that aren't seriously cutting spending budgets while still claiming a collective increase in production for 2015 as well. While the math on that may not compute to you, don't worry; I would surmise that it doesn't much compute for those who are reporting it either.

Figure 7-2:
2015 U.S. Shale Spending Budgets
(Courtesy RBN Energy)

Company Name	Basin	Capex 2014 Estimate ($ million)	Capex 2015 Guidance ($million)	% Change	Rig Count 2014	Rig Count 2015	% Change	Oil Production 2014 (Mboe/d)	Oil Production 2015 Guidance (Mboe/d)	% Change
American Eagle Energy Co	Bakken	115	5	-96%	1	0	-100%	2	N/A	
Emerald Oil Inc	Bakken	250	72	-71%	3	1	-67%	3	4	30%
Oasis Petroleum Inc	Bakken	1425	800	-44%	16	6	-63%	40	43	8%
Continental Resources Inc	Bakken / SCOOP	4550	2700	-41%	50	31	-38%	121	143	18%
Linn Energy LLC	California/Green River/E. TX	1550	730	-53%	N/A	N/A		73	63	-14%
Swift Energy Co	Eagle Ford	395	113	-71%	N/A	N/A		N/A	N/A	
Sanchez Energy	Eagle Ford	870	625	-28%	8	4	-50%	17	18	6%
Comstock Resources Inc	Eagle Ford /TMS/Haynesville	580	307	-47%	5	2	-60%	12	10	-15%
Halcon Resources	Eagle Ford/Bakken	1100	400	-64%	8	3	-63%	36	36	0%
Marthon Oil Corp	Global	5500	4400	-20%	N/A	N/A		N/A	N/A	
Conoco Phillips	Global	16875	13500	-20%	N/A	N/A		N/A	N/A	
REX Energy Corp	Marcellus/Utica	358	200	-44%	3	N/A		N/A	N/A	
Chaparral Energy LLC	Mid-Con	671	336	-50%	10	5	-50%	17	17	0%
PDC Energy Inc	Niobrara/Utica	637	557	-13%	6	5	-17%	13	17	36%
Diamondback Energy	Permian	450	425	-6%	6	3	-50%	N/A	N/A	
Concho Resources	Permian	2600	2000	-23%	36	26	-28%	71	73	2%
Approach Resources Inc	Permian	400	180	-55%	3	1	-67%	6	6	4%
Laredo Petroleum Inc	Permian	1100	525	-52%	14	5	-64%	18	21	12%
Rosetta Resources	Permian/ Eagle Ford	1200	750	-38%	7	4	-43%	19	21	10%
Encana Corp	Permian/ Eagle Ford	2550	2800	10%	36	26	-28%	119	150	26%
Matador Resources	Permian/Eagle Ford	570	350	-39%	5	3	-40%	8	4	-50%
Breitbrun Energy Partners	Permian/Mid-Con	375	200	-47%	N/A	N/A		22	31	41%
Abraxus Petroleum Corp	TMS	190	54	-72%	N/A	1		4	6	53%
Goodrich Petroleum Corp	TMS	350	175	-50%	4	2	-50%	5	6	36%
Total		44661	32204	-28%	221	128	-42%	606	669	10%

And here's the hallucination as I see it: somehow, every oil company in this extensive list and beyond believes that taking care of its individual corporate responsibility and balance sheet is all that is on its "to-do" list. Only a handful of oil companies (which I'll describe in the addendum, when I find the ones worthy of investment) is viewing the shale oil glut and frantic drilling schedule as an industry-wide issue to be solved collectively. Meanwhile, each one of them is individually planning on more oil production for 2015 and again for 2016. To put it more succinctly, each one of them is assiduously planning—not for itself and what it will take to rebalance shale production—but for the distress and demise of 'the other guy.' It is every single CEO's hope that it will be 'the other guy' who misses on production estimates and the prayer of every oil chief that it will be 'the other guy' whose abandonment of wells leads to less oil. Individually, it does show great confidence in your own company. But collectively, it's preposterous.

More preposterous is an outlier company like Encana, whose hallucinations led to even more bright optimism. For 2015, the Canadian natural gas behemoth decided not to cut spending at all, taking a complete blind eye towards collapsing prices. Instead, it chose to increase spending for 2015 from $2.55b to $2.8b. In this strategy, Encana is virtually alone in the oil space. CEO Doug Suttles has called the oil drop merely an "annoyance, but not threatening" and is continuing with his two-year plan to increase Encana's ratio of oil production from natural gas.

What made Encana so special? Why was it alone choosing to step on the accelerator while virtually everyone else was feathering the brakes? Well, it probably had a bit to do with Suttles' mistimed buy of Athlon Energy, a Permian basin start-up company that rocketed in share price in its less-than-two-year life span. In September 2014, Encana had the idea to buy Athlon for an astounding $5.9 billion, paying more than $58 a share for the fledgling company. That buy should have been accepted as a monumental error in timing, but instead has seemed to fuel the Encana fantasy. But if you've bought the top of the oil market, as Encana's Doug Suttles has, then why not—I suppose it makes perfect sense to double down and ignore collapsing oil and gas markets going forward. Encana plans to increase oil production by 26% in 2015.

Even OPEC's Secretary General Abdullah El-Badri began calling a bottom in oil prices in January 2015 and was expecting a recovery in the near future. Oil billionaire Boone Pickens has been vocal in his agreement on the 'self-correcting' nature of the oil markets as well. Their optimism is easy to understand, and I'll talk (in Chapter 8) about the next oil boom that seems so self-evident to these men.

Although spending cuts have no immediate effect on production, they do have an immediate effect on the number of working oil wells. As oil companies begin to hunker down for the long, lonely winter of cheap oil, they take a biased look towards current projects producing oil as well as planned new ones. As CEOs begin to 'circle the wagons,' they naturally pick out their most profitable projects with their strongest recovery rates and cheapest costs per barrel and concentrate their remaining capital on them. The least-efficient wells, or those that are at or near the end of their working life, will be jettisoned that much more quickly.

Another symptom in Phase I of the oil bust is a collapse in what is called *the rig count*. The number of working rigs in the U.S. is tracked precisely by Baker Hughes, an oil services company recently acquired by Halliburton. Rig counts have become a more critical metric since the rise in U.S. shale because of a shale well's typically fast decay rate. Because so much of the useful life of a well is overwhelmingly front-loaded, a deep discount in the oil price can have immediate effect on whether a project is abandoned in its 4th or 5th year, when remaining oil is minimal. It can also, obviously, stop the beginning of new projects if lease holders suddenly are realizing less than break-even prices for crude, as is the case now with hundreds of planned projects across the U.S. For the first several months of the shale bust, rig counts dropped as much as 200 a month, an enormous amount considering that even at its height, the U.S. had at most approximately 2000 working rotary rigs.

Figure 7-3:
Comparison of Oil Price with Rig Counts

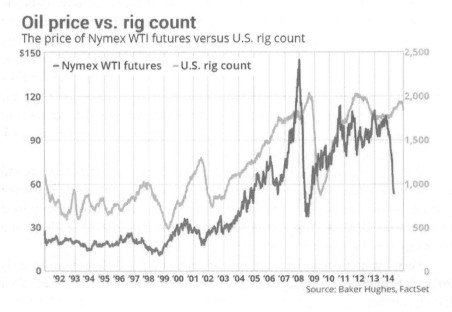

Source: Baker Hughes, FactSet

But this rapid drop in the number of rigs is nothing to be overwhelmed by. It is a very early 'weeding out' of the most inefficient and expensive projects in the portfolios of the marginal U.S. E+P players. This separation of the wheat from the chaff of oil wells is only another early indication of Phase I of the oil bust, as it does little to affect production in the short-term while chopping more immediate top-line costs for oil companies rather effectively.

It is in the long term when these reductions in marginal wells will be felt in production targets, but of course at this early stage in the crude bust, oil companies are less concerned about this; their priorities are in surviving to see the next year. After all, you can't be much concerned with quarterly reports 6 or 7 quarters in the future if you're not around to give them. In fact, rig counts could easily drop below 1,000 without much concurrent decrease in production, but they will have a more immediate effect on the companies that service those wells and the people employed there. And that leads us to Phase II of the shale bust timeline.

Phase II: The Capital Chase: Cutting Jobs, Raising Money

Phase II of the shale bust involves some far nastier consequences than a few slashed budgets and cutting of some marginal rigs. Cutting costs and capex budgets in a low oil environment is an obvious and relatively benign move for oil companies to make. Slashing jobs in such an environment, however, is another matter entirely. Cutting jobs requires a real sense of the long-term difficulties that are likely: putting people out of work—particularly highly skilled, experienced people—is something no company looks forward to. There are severance and pension issues, of course, but slashing a workforce leaves a bad taste not only among those who get fired, but among those who remain.

Also, reconstituting a qualified workforce when economics turn around can be equally challenging. When money is cut, nobody gets hurt. But when people get cut, the business itself can be mortally wounded. Cutting jobs is an indication that the management thinks things are going to be depressed for many months, and probably years.

Very few companies have cut jobs so far in 2015. The largest, as of early 2015, is Schlumberger, which slashed 9,000 jobs in January. Another 1,000 jobs have been lost so far at Halliburton. This is merely the tip of what is going to be a very powerful iceberg of job contraction here in the U.S. oil and gas sector. Of the 6 million jobs created in this country since 2009, fully 1.2 million have been attributed to the energy sector and the bonanza of cutting full-time positions and hundreds of thousands more jobs lost before this shale bust is fully spent.

The value of these jobs will have an increasingly negative impact on the U.S. economy at large. Jobs lost in oil services are not low-paying Wal-Mart or McDonald's jobs. They are the jobs of rig workers, pipefitters, geologists, dispatchers, truck drivers, and machinery operators—all representing relatively high-paying middle-class employment that support families. Job losses are a concrete indicator that the shale bust is well under way and will be an unfortunate but necessary indicator that low oil prices are being fully digested in the oil sector.

But a second set of indicators will show when we've entered Phase II of the shale bust. For many of the marginal shale players in the U.S., job losses won't be enough to stem the cash flow losses from low oil prices. Those companies will need new capital infusions if they want to survive. Cash can come in three ways: internally, from a new issue of bonds or a stock secondary; from a sale of assets; or from an outright merger or sale of the company.

A stock secondary or new bond issue is a luxury that will be reserved only for the very best of the oil companies. And by *best*, I mean those with bankable assets that have still managed to retain relatively conservatively leveraged balance sheets. In every new bond issue or secondary, you still have to sell the value of the company and its long-term viability to institutional and independent investors. This will prove more difficult to anyone except the 'cream' of shale players. To those that have bankruptcy risk and can do it, a new bond issue or a stock secondary can be a lifesaver.

Still, a new issue or secondary carries a huge punishment with it. Resorting to a secondary in a depressed oil world dilutes shares and potential earnings at the worst possible time.

Look at the case of Southwestern Energy (SWN). Throughout 2014, Southwestern, despite a very strong balance sheet and some of the lowest oil and gas recovery rates in the sector, decided to embark on a large expansion plan. Instead of holding steady in production, increasing efficiencies, and waiting for markets to turn favorably, the company viewed the depressed natural gas and oil price as an opportunity to increase its asset base, particularly in the Marcellus shale formation of Pennsylvania. In March 2014, it began by buying Niobrara assets in Colorado from Quicksilver Resource for $180 million. It followed that up with a partial purchase of Statoil's natural gas assets in West Virginia and Pennsylvania for $365 million, and it bought midstream assets from WPX Energy for $288 million in December 2014. But the real blockbuster move was Southwestern's buy of almost $5.4 billion of Chesapeake Energy's prime Marcellus acreage at a fairly wide premium, despite the depressed state of the markets at the time. The hallucination for Southwestern was the same as for so many others in the space—that depressed oil and gas prices were going to be only a short-term blip on the radar and represented an opportunity for the next up cycle to come.

But timing is everything. Unfortunately for Southwestern, the oil and gas markets have not recovered in time to restore an adequate company cash flow, made much more difficult by the spending spree it went on in 2014. Big acquisitions require big spending plans; obviously, it makes absolutely no sense to buy assets (overleveraging your company in the process) and not proceed in developing them. And Southwestern needed money to do that.

Consequently, in January 2015, Southwestern was forced into a 26 million-share secondary offering of new stock, raising almost $6 billion of new capital for the company. The $23 share price represented a 6-year low in the price of the stock, leaving billions of dollars unrealized because of the poor timing of the deal. Yet we still should consider Southwestern one of the lucky ones, as it was easily able to find more than enough enthusiasm among investors for its $6 billion secondary to be oversubscribed. Investors are still finding a lot of value in even distressed dilutive shares of oil companies with strong assets, like Southwestern. The market has seen several other oil companies who have managed to find support for successful stock secondaries in this very early stage of refinancing rounds, including Diamondback Energy (a dedicated Permian play producer), Bonanza Creek Energy, and Noble Energy (a Niobrara shale player).

Less lucky was Linn Energy, a U.S. E+P player structured as a master limited partnership (MLP). Linn was already toeing a very fine line for a shale producer, in that its MLP structure required it to deliver large distributions to its shareholders. The cash drain for Linn because of this type of structure has to be a more difficult proposition as opposed to any other 'regular' C-class energy company pulling oil out of the ground, so the crude drop certainly could have concerned the leadership at Linn Energy more than elsewhere.

Linn's solution, however, wasn't a particularly happy one. In early January 2015, Linn entered into a financing agreement with Blackstone partners, the large publicly traded private equity firm, for up to $500 million of capital to develop new Linn properties. The downside was in delivering to Blackstone the promise of 85% of the proceeds from these new assets, a tremendous premium for a rather measly half a billion dollars of commitments. It assures two things for Linn: that the company will survive to see through the winter of $50 oil, but also that it won't make much to keep for itself in the next few years on new production that it has promised. For Linn, this looks like a deal made with the devil; for Blackstone, it looks utterly fantastic.

Whichever way that marginal U.S. shale players do it, there has to be a rash of these kinds of deals, not just the one or two I've mentioned here. The financing issues facing Southwestern Energy and Linn aren't in any way unique to them; it was only their unique circumstances that impelled them to hit the panic button first. Many more companies will look to follow their leads in refinancing before we've likely seen the end of Phase II of the shale bust.

Phase III: Consolidation of Asset Ownership

Phase III, the final stage of the U.S. shale oil bust, is a continuation of Phase II in that the search for cash flow becomes more critical. In Phase III, not only do refinancings from fresh bond issues and stock secondary offerings continue, and the capital comes not only from private equity or other private interests where the assets deserve it, but a more outright selling of prime assets to stave off bond defaults and bankruptcy occurs. What causes this more dire stage to begin is the onset of the production wall that we've discussed in the previous chapter finally hitting. At some point, the connection between decreasing money spent and rigs working translates into real and a measurable lowering of production levels. And for those where the fantasy explodes first, there will need to be outright sales of assets to keep the lights on. Many of the distressed asset hedge funds have been interested in the opportunities presented by this third phase and will be searching out the oil companies most likely to fall into this situation.

That type of company is actually rather easy to spot: its financial position will be unsustainably leveraged for a low oil environment, yet it will concurrently have some very respected reserve assets. Two companies that come to mind in this mold are Halcon Resources and Sandridge Resources, both with difficult bond positions trading under 75 cents on the dollar and yielding in the high teens. Neither of these companies are 'lost causes,' however. The reason both of these players are very interesting to distressed bond traders are that both have tremendous assets that will be easy to monetize when the time comes: Halcon owns prime acreage in the western Williams county of North Dakota of the Bakken and Sandridge has great potential acreage in the Tuscaloosa Marine Shale in Louisiana. Both sets of acreage are uneconomic for further development with oil prices this low, but they would be terrific assets to have 'in the quiver' for a larger oil company looking to buy growth on the cheap—and for when oil prices ultimately rally.

And for those hedge funds that have been scouring this landscape for candidate companies who will need to sell assets, it is in their bonds that much of the investment is being done. It is possible for common shares in a number of these marginal E+P players to go to zero while the bondholders are still made whole. In the sale of assets, or even in the full sale of the company itself, is the first promise to satisfy the debt. GSO Capital Partners, the credit arm of Blackstone partners, is quickly assembling a new $1 billion fund exclusively for the purchase of distressed oil company corporate bonds. Blackstone has an additional advantage in this game of bond buying on the cheap: with its financing arm on the other side of the deal holding a carrot, GSO can add additional pressure on distressed companies to accelerate asset sales in order to avoid a default. Blackstone is certainly not alone in seeking the opportunity from distressed oil companies. Warburg Pincus and Carlyle Group are two other huge private equity players roaming the range for distressed bonds to buy. This is another opportunity that private equity is preparing to exploit fully in the coming phase III of the shale bust.

Despite this hovering of the 'vultures' over the carcasses of distressed U.S. E+Ps, this last phase of asset sales is a necessary market weeding out of the weakest players in the shale game. However, even more must happen before we know that the bust is finally nearing its end.

Another possible outcome for overleveraged, distressed oil companies could be a buyout by a larger company, most likely one of the four mega-cap integrated oil companies: Exxon Mobil, Chevron, Conoco-Phillips, or Royal Dutch Shell. Large integrated oil companies have been faced with a particular challenge in the last several years of rising costs to find and implement new production. In the energy business, Wall Street is never satisfied with a company that just stands still on production, whether large or small; growth remains one of the most important metrics that spurs robust share prices.

In the never-ending chase for production growth, the point in the big drop in oil prices hasn't been lost on the majors. They know that low oil prices force smaller oil companies towards far more stressed capital positions than they must bear. This presents for them an opportunity that the 'big boys' have not seen since the late 90s, when mega-cap oil companies made very big consolidation deals to capture cheap future growth. During that era of consolidation, Exxon merged with Mobil, BP bought Amoco, and Chevron bought Texaco. In these towering deals, majors bought future production through the takeover of weaker, more debt-ridden producers. This time around, the opportunities are no different, and the majors are focused for a similar buying spree, even if the magnitude of perhaps an Exxon and Mobil oil merger doesn't quite exist.

In the coming merger/buyout frenzy, shale oil assets will figure most prominently. Rex Tillerson, CEO of Exxon, has made clear in a few rare moments of on-air candor Exxon's desire during this market downturn to purchase struggling oil companies with quality assets, particularly those with shale: "We stay very alert to value propositions," Exxon said on its 2014 4th quarter call. "We'll pursue only those acquisitions that we think have ultimate strategic value and will benefit our long-term reserves. We're really looking for something that upgrades our portfolio and adds to our potential." Translation: With strong natural gas and conventional assets, liquids and crude will be the focus for Exxon on a potential acquisition during this latest round of low oil prices. With a cash position stronger than anyone else in the industry and a war chest to leverage well upwards of $100b, Exxon could easily target some of the larger crude-focused large-cap U.S. companies, including Anadarko (APC), Continental (CLR), or Hess (HES).

Shell, on the other hand, has made its big move already, buying British natural gas and LNG giant BG Group in a $70b mega deal in March 2015. Despite paying a 50% premium for the distressed company, Shell still managed to buy BG at 7-year lows for the stock and increase their combined production potential to 16.7b barrels of oil equivalent (BOE) and deliver a reserves-to-production ratio of 12.4 years—a tremendous example of buying future production growth, even if it wasn't entirely on the cheap. Despite the premium that Shell paid, it was clearly itchy to take advantage of the depressed share prices that low oil and gas had created. Royal Dutch

Shell was first to the takeover party, perhaps prematurely so in early 2015—at least certainly Exxon and Chevron hope that better opportunities will emerge further down the road.

That's because premiums for oil companies have continued in the share prices of other shale- and liquids-focused producers and haven't yet caused the avalanche of M&A as of April 2015, frankly surprising me and I think the majors as well. Investors seem to continue to want to overpay for oil stocks, much as Shell seemed to want to overpay for BG Group: many of the mini-majors I cited as potential targets for Exxon are trading at prices equivalent for oil barrels selling for $80-85, not for the $55 where oil is now hovering. But sector rotation or other optimism in oil companies notwithstanding, several more quarters of low oil prices and reduced revenues will ultimately impact these share prices, bringing them back into line and more apt for a "reasonable premium" takeover.

Take Whiting Petroleum (WLL), a dedicated Bakken producer, as an example. On March 9, 2015, its leaders announced that they preferred to find a buyer for their struggling company, foregoing other weaker capital-raising options that would dilute value and make them less appetizing a target. Although Exxon was named as a likely suitor, meeting their assumed need for quality shale assets, neither Exxon nor anyone else came forward with a satisfactory bid for the company. Whiting ultimately gave up its search for a buyer on March 26th, choosing to raise capital as so many other shale players had, with its own secondary stock offering. Despite the tasty Bakken assets that Whiting controls, it became clear that Exxon and others felt Whiting's valuation far too rich to buy. Exxon and other mega-majors are banking that the opportunity remains down the road to make big consolidation moves as Shell has done—but at a far cheaper price. Only time will tell if they will be proven right.

Finally, for those companies that cannot either find financing and whose assets aren't particularly compelling for a larger oil company or private equity firm to scoop up, an outright bankruptcy could occur. It's hard to know who will ultimately disappear in this rearrangement of shale players, but I believe at least a dozen smaller-cap companies will ultimately fold completely, with their assets remaining on the books of the regional banks that have financed them, waiting for a buyer. Phase III of the shale bust for these marginal players and their shareholders will be ugly, indeed.

However, two very important things for the future of energy in the U.S. will be accomplished in this final stage of the shale bust. First, the rearrangement of shale assets will move from relatively weak hands into far stronger ones, with the capabilities to withstand tough challenges in oil market cycles without resorting to hugely dilutive secondary offerings or disadvantaged financing arrangements.

And second, the results of this oil market Darwinism will result in a real drop in U.S. oil production. As the most marginal players fold and the lesser players sell assets that get put on a shelf (to enhance future production) instead of being actively developed, the straight-up progression of U.S. production from shale will finally level off, and then, at last, begin to drop. Even now, the EIA does not expect this to happen. And if you take its current projections at face value, the EIA doesn't expect it ever to happen. Of course, the EIA is wrong—it has to be. And that slackening of production and finally retreat of barrels won't happen very quickly. At best, I do not expect even a leveling off in supplies at least until the 4th quarter of 2015 and the beginnings of a real and measurable drop in production until the 2nd quarter of 2016.

All three of these stages of reconstruction inside the oil industry needs to occur, and some pretty dramatic blood needs to be spilled before we can mark the beginning of the end of the shale bust. There will be the large-scale movement of oil assets from the weakest hands through sales and distressed partnerships. Those that cannot restructure will either be sold or go broke. Major oil companies will begin to consolidate as they did during the last oil bust in the late 90s. And finally, rig counts that already have dropped by more than 40% will translate into a real drop in oil production in the U.S. to far less frantic levels that we have currently in 2015. The EIA will be proven wrong in its predictions for continuing increases in U.S. production, as it seems many others expect as well. Only then will the prerequisites be in place for the next oil boom to start.

Chapter 8:

THE NEXT BOOM

Markets are forward looking. We hear that all the time. What people mean by that isn't meant to be cryptic; there are always speculators constantly roaming the markets for opportunities, trying to 'jump ahead' of the next major trend. Many of them are very smart, making their livings from predictions and actually getting many of them right. In the shale bust, almost every one of them is going to get it right because it is impossible for oil to stay below $65 for very long.

There are a handful of talking heads and analysts who have surprisingly spoken about the crash in oil prices in 2014 heralding a 'new era,' where fossil fuels will never again be the singular driver of energy economies they currently are. In October 2014, Dennis Gartman, a lifetime commodities expert and publisher of the respected *Gartman Letter*, said on CNBC that oil's price demise would accompany its economic demise as well. "It's going the way of whale oil," he pronounced, comparing crude to another long-obsolete source of fuel and predicting that oil would ultimately reach $10 a barrel.

Dennis's point of view is very rare indeed. I see a more random but still logical progression of causes and effects in this latest bust cycle. And from that progression of facts, my conclusion is that this bust cycle does not end crude oil's reign as the most important energy source on the planet. In fact, it convinces me that this bust will surely lead to another fantastic boom.

In this point of view, I am hardly in the minority. Almost every analyst, energy CEO, and writing observer of the energy world seems to see it coming as an inevitable, almost well-trodden ending to the most stereotypically plotted mystery yarn. Although they all see a new rise in prices, they don't agree on the speed, shape, or ultimate force of the next rally to come. Some see the next rise in prices as a moderate one, where financial forces and fundamentals slowly glide back into easy equilibrium of $75-$80 oil, a nice profitable level for much of current production, and above breakeven prices for critical marginal barrels. Others foresee a much more violent rebound, with prices greatly overshooting any kind of reasonable fundamental price,

93

with some (including the Secretary General of OPEC El-Badri) seeing a brand new price high approaching $200 a barrel.

Count me overwhelmingly in this latter camp. Having witnessed the many ups and downs of oil over the decades, it would be foolish to assume that the next boom won't have all of the excesses of the previous ones. If this next move up takes a now-familiar course (including the same kind of pricing excesses and behaviors I've witnessed now so many times before) and if all the producers, consumers, governments, traders, hedge funds, algorithmic black boxes, and media outlets surrounding the oil markets do precisely what they've been so painstakingly built to do, then this next boom has all the likelihood of being the most overblown yet, making even 2007's $145 top price seem mild.

In other words, *get ready.*

How will this turnaround make itself known? When will we know when we've really entered a new boom cycle and not just a retracement to 'normal' levels? And, much more important for investment and policy decisions, how long will it take before it begins, how high does it go, and how long does it last? Let's try to put some boundaries around some of these questions.

Demand Provides the Spark

Here's a place to start the analysis—in the continuing rise of oil demand globally, as shown in Figure 8-1.

Figure 8-1:
Growing Oil Demand

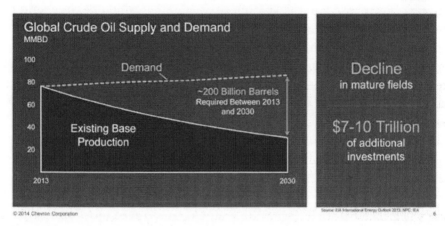

Source: Chevron Corporation Investor Presentation.

Now, how simple is that? This elegant slide from Chevron's investor conference charts the average decline rate of currently producing assets from 2013 through 2030, using a very conservative 5% average decay rate for production. Concurrently, Chevron drew an upwards sloping line representing an (exceedingly!) conservative demand curve for oil for the next 15 years, showing an increase of barely 5 million barrels a day. (In contrast, I would be shocked—as would the IEA, OPEC, and just about every other oil company—if the number weren't at least twice that.) Still, with Chevron's very conservative calculations, one immediately comes to a very sharp deficit in the oil markets of more than 40 million barrels a day at the end of the curve, for a total deficit of 200 billion barrels of oil over the next 15 years—that is, if all new exploration were to flat out stop today. It is a hyperbolic chart, obviously, but valuable.

Chevron uses this very impactful slide as part of its investor presentations to make a point about the requirements of continued development spending: Chevron estimates that $10 trillion will need to be spent to develop the barrels necessary to merely keep up with demand increases that are accompanying the natural decline of existing wells.

I draw a different point from it. Figure 8-1 is describing production declines when current wells continue to perform, but what would happen to this chart if current wells were forced to curtail their production, or shut down altogether? The slope on declining available barrels would be far steeper, for a start. The shortfall one would find as time moves forward would be far greater, and the amount of money that would be needed to be spent to 'get back to even' would exponentially rise.

This is precisely what is going to be the inevitable reaction from the current massive slashing of capex across the industry and the concurrent drop in rigs. As of March 2015, rig counts are down an unprecedented 480 since December 2014. (Late addition: US rig count has dropped close to 1000 as of May 2015.) So far, of course, production has continued to increase despite this, but we now know this is a hallucination, a phantom that cannot last and whose rebound will necessarily be huge. We know that the remaining wells operating during the shale bust are being pumped frantically, but 'efficiency gains' can get you only so far. Once those wells start to show major declines, as they are going to do even more quickly than was originally planned, that production 'brick wall' I mention in Chapter 3 on shale scalability is going to start to approach in a fantastically scary hurry. I have avoided the obviously concurrent declines that must accompany Canadian oil sands mining and in deep-water projects particularly, but these also will see contraction throughout 2015 and 2016 and add to that inevitable shortfall to come.

Andrew Hall, perhaps the most famous oil trader in the world, has remained mostly silent since collecting his side-by-side $100 million bonuses from trading oil for Phibro, one of the oldest and best respected commodity trading firms, which was then owned by Citibank. Since curtailing his work at Phibro, he has started his own oil hedge fund, Astenbeck Capital, again using the singular strategy that made Mr. Hall so famous and so wealthy. Although his trading strategy is more complex than I will describe it, Hall has been almost maniacally bullish on oil, most recently because he believed (as I do) that shale resources are far less bottomless than most other analysts and that even with advancing technology techniques, there will be a big drop-off in recovery rates far sooner than most others predict.

The performance of Astenbeck could not have been good during the downturn in oil prices in 2014, but in early 2015, after formally leaving Phibro entirely, Mr. Hall came out of hiding to again predict a major demand-based spike in oil prices: "Prices at current levels (or lower) are not sustainable for very long," Hall wrote in his yearly letter to investors. "The current surplus could thus easily set the stage for a future deficit." Mr. Hall predicts both an increase of demand from lower oil prices, but also a very significant fall in production: he believes 2.4 million barrels a day of conventional oil is likely to disappear. Further, he accentuates the strength of shale producers as swing producers by noting the differences between 2015 and 1986, the last time a major drop in prices inspired a demand-based rally.

The most important difference for Hall, according to his end of 2014 letter, is that in 1986, OPEC had about 25% of spare capacity, meaning almost instantaneous resources to increase supply by another quarter of their production. The true amount of Saudi Arabia's and OPEC's spare capacity is a topic of some debate, but all agree that the spigots could not be increased to flow by anywhere near that much today. "Today's surplus is only 2% higher than global oil consumption, and it will have dissipated by the end of the year, if not sooner," he opined.

I could not agree more with Mr. Hall. And his track record of success is a nice indicator of his ability to see the future big moves in the oil market.

Andrew Hall may be positioning himself now for the next coming boom cycle, but the market will need more than the predictions of some good traders to turn around. One thing that absolutely must happen is a real and measurable leveling off of production here in the U.S. Early in the bust phase for shale, with crude prices, budgets, and rig counts collapsing, I was of the opinion that indeed, production cuts would come a whole lot sooner than either the EIA or most of the bank analysts believed was possible. But I've been impressed by the free flow of capital that has come in to the markets looking to 'save' shale oil companies from their excesses, and slowing what I thought would be a violent progression of bond defaults and outright bankruptcies.

In a recent note on the state of E+P, Morgan Stanley also noted the trend, when one of its analysts, Evan Calio, wrote:

"Secondary offerings have been positively received by investors as a means to shore up balance sheets and pre-fund drilling programs in light of falling crude prices. Secondary offerings remain a logical way to delever [a financial term meaning to reduce debt], but also has *the potential to extend the trough rather than hasten its arrival.*" (emphasis mine).

In other words, there is too much money still chasing oil for a quick weeding out of the weaklings. We might see a longer period of 'survivability' before the real wall hits.

But that wall is most definitely out there. Even with a capital infusion, far too many companies will just have to cry uncle at some point as oil prices remain low. And the 'Catch-22' is that oil prices will stay low as long as no one cries uncle. Then, one day, it will all come apart.

When will that be? If shale decline rates remain the same, I'm guessing not longer than in the 4th quarter of 2015. By the 2nd quarter of 2016, the coming shortage should be evident to everyone. Of course, once it starts, it will be an avalanche of production shortfalls that will quickly wipe out any domestic gluts—and they won't be able to be replaced. There will be no new spigot to turn on. That should make for a hell of a U.S. Presidential election season.

And it is precisely what Mr. Hall is counting on.

What other pressures, of the 5 major pressures I outlined on oil, are likely to dissipate enough to allow for a new boom cycle? And which of those other pressures might actually turn around completely, and move from anchor to engine to put wind into the sails of a new boom?

I see a concrete drop in U.S. production as the key pivot point around which many of the other pressures are likely to be relieved. First, we'll see those numbers level off and begin to decline, but then other forces that are ready to 'take advantage' in varying ways of the coming supply shortfall will certainly follow.

First to follow, I believe will likely be Saudi Arabia and OPEC. I imagine that the internal conversations even now between the Saudis and other OPEC members are entirely about the real potential and opportunity that will arise when this inevitable U.S. production shortfall hits. Oil economics truly operate on a razor's edge: with a global production of 92 million barrels a day and a demand for almost every single one of those barrels, even the slightest discrepancy on the supply side can have a monumental impact on price. We remember in 2010 how even the smallest 1 million barrel supply of the Libyans coming offline during their civil war was enough to make oil rally significantly above $110 a barrel, even as the Saudis promised added barrels to offset the shortfall. So imagine what the initial price of oil might get to when U.S. production ratchets back by two or three hundred thousand barrels, or even perhaps a million barrels.

Now imagine what might happen if the Saudis decided that this moment of supply shortfall from U.S. producers around the 2nd quarter of 2016 was suddenly the perfect strategic moment to suggest a Cartel-wide production cut, as so many OPEC members have so vigorously lobbied for since November 2014. Or imagine what might happen if the Saudis unilaterally decided to reestablish their firm grip on the global oil markets by unilaterally dropping production by a half million or million barrels a day. The secondary push higher on prices would be astronomical. A correctly timed production cut by the Saudis would destroy the 'end of OPEC' pronouncements being claimed by several analysts in recent weeks and put the cartel again at the fulcrum point of world pricing. It is this master stroke to their master plan that I believe the Saudis are lying in wait to apply, pushing prices astronomically higher at a time when they alone have the resources to fully service the global demand—or not. In a year, cartel members will be able to recoup all the losses they bore during the collapse. And OPEC's grip on global oil will be stronger than ever before.

Is there anything else might add fuel to this coming fire?

The Dollar Turns

The dollar is certainly 'due' for a turnaround, or at least for a respite from the very steady move upwards that it has enjoyed, as shown in Figure 8-2.

Figure 8-2:
U.S. Dollar Index 2014-2015

You may not know much about trading or about charting. And although the momentum of this chart may still look very much on an upwards path and nothing to be trifled with (or bet against), it's also simply impossible for anything—especially a *currency*—to continue to move with this much power and unilateral direction. I'll admit to having little expertise on the trading of the U.S. dollar, but I do know that charts like this do not last forever.

When might this chart change? Again, having little unique insight into Fed policy and bond markets and the inside plans of the ECB and Bank of Japan, I hesitate to predict. But can the dollar continue to move like this for more than another year? My trading experience says no. There seems a natural boundary as the dollar reaches parity with the Euro that is difficult to breach. At these lofty levels however, any turnaround in the dollar index should have an immediate positive impact on oil prices, and it should come at just about the right time—at the end of 2015/start of 2016.

European Growth Recovers

Chinese and European growth and where that might be in 2016 or 2017 is even more difficult for me as an oil guy to try and judge, but only the latest news tells me things might be getting better there as well coming into 2016 and beyond. If the EU holds together (which now seems more likely than not), it is clear that the slow but steady abandonment of economic austerity as the lone 'correct' path to recovery force-feeds liquidity and growth into Europe. Whether or not you are in agreement with this new 'old' path to recovery, it's likely to inspire better numbers in the next few years.

Oil's Endless Bid Returns

Lastly, there is the one financial factor that matters so much but is casually ignored and almost never discussed (except, it seems, by me): the speculative appetite for oil investment. The Bank for International Settlement (BIS, which is known as the central bankers' bank) released a report in February 2015 commenting on the nature of the crude collapse. It noted that the fundamental changes in supply and demand did not differ markedly from expectations, and they fall short of providing a satisfactory explanation for the abrupt collapse in prices. The BIS did not note the exit of investment bank interest in oil as I do, but the BIS report commented that oil's price volatility is normally less common among commodities and more often associated with financial assets.

And like any other financial asset, it is ultimately the number of buyers and sellers that moves the markets and sets the price. In oil, we have seen the fast exit of a huge class of buyers (i.e., retail and institutional investors) leaving many of the sellers without matches on the other side or without matchmakers who can find them.

Who will be the next matchmaker in an oil market that has every rocket staged and only needs a new supply of buyers to catapult prices higher, maybe higher than ever before?

This is the question that fascinates me the most, because I know that opportunity is not one that will likely be missed. Someone will be ready to come forward and 'sell' oil as an asset to be owned again—marketing oil to pensions, endowments, family trusts, hedge funds, and individual investors. I'm just wondering who it will be. Will the investment banks try to 'get the band back together,' reestablishing their marketing departments and trading desks, even with the added burdens of Dodd-Frank and Basel III? I tend to doubt it. The decade prior to 2008 were the 'golden years' for these proprietary shops and they're not likely to be repeated. Even if the investment banks have the expertise and experience to succeed again, I suspect that too many watchful eyes will not allow a repeat performance.

So who will it be?

Could the more quiet and secretive private trading houses of Vitol, Mercuria, Glencore, and Trifigura want to venture into the dirty business of retail marketing? When the time arrives, they may try. But whomever it is, they would need to have at least a marginal connection to the oil business or to oil companies as clients and still be flying somewhat under the radar of new financial restrictions and capital constraints. That requirement eliminates insurance companies, because they have caught the target bull's eye, courtesy of AIG's excesses during the financial crisis. And although they've been vocal in their complaints about new regulations and capital requirements, complaints won't change the laws back to the free-wheeling days of 2006.

How about the private equity groups? Their reputations on Wall Street are colossal; they seemingly can raise billions from investors at any moment; they command the bond markets as well as the equity markets from their deep capital perch, and they have been expanding their reach and scope when others have been throttling back. Many of the largest private equity firms have been amassing huge war chests specifically to concentrate on energy assets. Warburg Pincus has a $4b fund that it began in October 2014. Carlyle Group is putting together a total of $8 billion to shop with. There's also Apollo Global Management, already deep in the oil patch for years, and certainly Blackstone Group as well. Both of these organizations have been licking their chops at the prospect of cherry picking distressed assets in the oil patch during the crude collapse. Greg Beard, head of energy investing for Apollo, opined in February 2015 that the disaster in oil was only beginning. In this prediction, he could be right; however, publicly saying it sounds more like the prayer of a wolf holding a match and a can of lighter fluid just waiting for the fire sale to start.

Once these companies have assembled their juicy portfolios of picked-over shale resources from the limping and outright dying in the oil patch, what better way would there be to accelerate their value and monetization than by supporting the fast and 'enthusiastic' rise of oil prices, when that opportunity begins to show itself? New marketing and trading divisions inside companies like these could do quite a bit to add capital (and buyers) to an oil market just starting to get ripe again. PE firms have somehow avoided the scrutiny of the regulators as well: they could walk into the oil trading and marketing business and impact it for a very long time before even attracting the attention of the CFTC, SEC and Justice Departments. To be frank, all of those agencies have their hands full already eyeing the insurance companies and the banks.

Of course, all of this is pure speculation on my part. But it's still fun. The one thing I'm convinced of is that when the oil market finally finds its fundamental legs in the midst of a systemic supply shortage, someone will be there to help inspire a skyrocketing price and make a Midas's fortune from it.

And, as usual, the benefits won't go to the guy filling his tank up at the pump.

Conclusions

In 2014, President Obama gave another speech, with energy as the side issue. To me, his administration has never been politically comfortable in discussing energy as a prime topic. On this occasion (as on so many), he reveled in quoting U.S. production numbers, which are stunning. This is a country that has nearly doubled its output in oil in 5 short years, and is now, according to several estimates, the number one producer of energy in the world. Of course, Mr. Obama has done little to make this amazing turnaround happen, yet in his speeches, he still appeals to take credit for the success.

In reality, he has been a determined foe of domestic energy development, including a tremendous open crackdown on coal, which is now slowly but surely going the way of the dodo-bird in generating electricity for our nation's grid. On natural gas, he has refused to openly support the conversion of transport (particularly trucks) to natural gas engines—a move that would truly go the longest way to making the U.S. energy independent. And on oil, Mr. Obama has kowtowed to the environmentalist base in his party by putting up every roadblock possible in the building of the Keystone pipeline. In the exploding world of horizontal drilling of shale, he has abdicated his leadership position completely, leaving production guidelines entirely in the hands of individual states. Because of his indifference, or more likely political need, we've seen a wide variance of development and oversight— from the almost Wild-West ease of exploration and production in Texas to the outright ban on fracking in New York State.

No matter where you fall on any of these issues, whether right or left, whether you agree with the President or find his stance merely gutless, this much is true: the United States is not one step closer to finding a unified energy policy that works, and the U.S.—despite its tremendous success with shale—is going to end up without the energy independence from foreign oil it craves. In my opinion, Washington and particularly the President are to blame for this.

That's more than a shame. It's a crime. The bonanza that is shale oil and gas and its promise of reasonable energy costs and independence from foreign influences is not an everlasting opportunity. It is going to come only once, and I could argue that its peak has come and gone already. Once these few very rich plays in Texas and North Dakota and variant minor ones in 5 or 6 other states are developed and drained, that's it. We're done, and the opportunity in shale oil will have passed. We've still got time, however, to craft a policy that takes advantage of our unique position with shale and prepares us for a quality energy path for both consumers and the oil industry for the next several decades, ultimately leading to a more sustainable energy future.

Yet oil's price volatility remains the singularly most difficult hurdle to overcome. If I've managed to prove one thing about energy, it is that *price means everything*, and you cannot craft a policy that delivers the U.S. a modicum of independence and security without a major bow to oil's price dynamics. Shale oil has now become entrenched as the 'swing barrel' source inside the global supply chain and therefore will be the most sensitive to price swings. But just because U.S. shale is now clearly the most sensitive does not mean it needs to be ratcheting from boom to bust over and over again, moving in massive, profit-soaked waves as prices increase and alternately suffering through contractions, job losses, and defaults when prices decline.

In January 2015, I was interviewed again by Chris Hayes on his MSNBC show, and he led into my segment on gas prices with a question: "I thought the purpose of the financial markets was to smooth out the variations in price; isn't that the reason they're supposed to exist?"

I grinned on the inside, maybe a bit on the outside, too. In my internal conversation, even as I delivered a simpler answer on air, I was thinking *yeah, right...how much time have you got, Chris?*

Yes, while stable pricing may be the 'advertised-to-the-public' appeal of the commodity markets, but no, this is not the outcome of platforms becoming ever more sophisticated and complex. It's quite the opposite. Markets aren't meant to smooth out variance and volatility; instead, they are the conduits for both. Financial markets give access to thousands upon thousands of players with no physical connection to the products that are being priced, and they are all engaged for only one reason: to make money on the movement in those prices. Not one of those financial players gives a hoot about stability. In fact, they all pray never to see it.

That truth about the oil market is both intractable and unchangeable. The idea of 'fixing the system' to remove volatility is something I thought a lot about during the aftermath of the financial crisis of 2008, but now believe is frankly an impossible task no longer worth considering. The system we've got has taken decades to develop and has spawned whole industries that employ hundreds of thousands of advisors, traders, regulators, clerks, secretaries, schedulers, risk managers, and so on. Every one of those participants has political power and a vested interest in seeing that system remain in place. Price volatility is something we're not only going to have to live with, but something we must get used to.

Yet the effects of financial price volatility needn't have such major consequences in the very short term for the shale industry, and they don't have to mess up the development of the unexpected godsend of shale oil either. Although we can't control or even predict the wild swings in oil's price, we can help control the volatility inside the industry itself with just a few added restrictions. Most important is how the limited resources in our shale plays continue to be developed in the future. The boom in shale perhaps didn't make it clear, but the recent bust cycle absolutely proves that who is developing our shale and how it's being developed is critical. And during the bust there appears to be the lone perfect opportunity to make those changes. I hope we will take it. A couple of suggestions are in order.

To start, *we absolutely need a unified national set of guidelines on shale drilling.* That's not as onerous a suggestion as it first sounds, but there are a few things that need uniformity across the country. Start with an industry standard on acreage leases that does not put scheduling for drilling at the whim of the oil company nor mandates immediate development from the lessee. Further standards on delay rentals on deferred drilling are needed (those charges to lessors for not developing well sites) and standards on which wells can be held on production (those wells that are being contractually forced to continue to pump despite negative economics). The forward momentum on drilling for shale oil cannot be done with a singular bow to profits alone; other national (particularly environmental) interests must also be taken into account, and in many cases may trump the rapacious instincts of both the oil company and the lease holder. That means an unequivocal national ban on the flaring of associated natural gas from shale oil wells—a rule I have long believed should be in place without exception or exemption.

Talking about flaring, it shouldn't matter how insignificant the amount of associated gas is coming from these shale oil wells, either. If you don't have the pipelines in place to transport and add that gas into the network as you drill for oil, you're just not ready yet to drill. Finally, we must now create a Federal regulatory structure that makes more uniform how wells are drilled and how they are fracked. I'm not talking about completely homogeneous and rigid requirements, as room must be left for further innovation in the science of horizontal drilling. But today, the variations in fracking operations are still all over the map and need tightening. The Obama administration recently took a small step in this direction by putting forward a few very conservative regulations for the fracking of shale that will initially apply only to drilling taking place on government leased acreage. These standards, put out in March 2015, were not surprisingly met with hoots of protest from oil and gas lobby groups. No matter: these initiatives should be furthered, made far stronger, and should ultimately extend beyond Federal lands to include all of the United States.

These ideas collectively make fracking more difficult and more expensive, it's true. But that's part of the point: making the procurement of oil from shale more costly is of paramount importance, and not only to incentivize the development of alternative energy sources that I wrote about in the Introduction. They will also aid in the necessary restructuring of shale assets and development responsibility that I wrote about as well.

These combined suggestions would serve to put a lot of pressure on the smaller, less-capitalized shale player and admittedly favors the larger, better-equipped, and better-financed E+Ps. It will help progress the restructuring process that the shale bust of 2014 started, by taking assets away from highly leveraged, marginal players and putting them in the hands of companies with stronger balance sheets. It also definitely increases development costs, but it also puts that development in the much more conservative hands of those who can better bear the risks of price volatility. These suggestions would help to ensure a safer and more equitable national development of shale resources. Finally, they will slow down the breakneck speed at which our shale oil is being taken out of the ground, saving it for a moment when it not only benefits the markets the most, but also when it benefits the developer the most. There's been a great American revolution of shale that has been started and carried out, at least up until now, by some singularly admirable entrepreneurs. They've created dozens of smaller and mid-cap energy companies with cheap debt and hard work and the kind of American spirit that all of us love to see and celebrate. But the time has come for these trailblazers to take their profits and step aside, for the sake of the nation.

By subtly changing the structure of shale oil activity through regulation as well as consolidation, we'll extend the benefits of the resource—not only for the long-term profit margins of oil companies in the slower, more conservative development schedule of slow growth, but also for consumers and for our economy. Further, it will allow our unique and once-in-a-lifetime shale oil resources to last several more decades than they are apt to last now, making a necessary transition to a renewable energy future based on solar energy a lot easier to reach. Our energy future, without these or any further standards, will find shale oil continuing to be drilled based solely on market forces of which we have no control; and production will forever be bouncing up and crashing down, dependent on these unpredictable financial inputs. When prices are low, major stresses of lost jobs and lower growth will burden the U.S. economy. And when prices are high, the incentive will be to simply drill it—and use it up—as fast as we can.

Neither makes any sense.

As long as I'm writing some ideas on how the development of U.S. energy might go forward from here, I'll add one idea, unlikely as it might be, whose time has undoubtedly come: a national gasoline tax. I've been accused during much of my career after leaving the floor and beginning oil analysis and column writing of being a perma-bull on oil. *Oil's Endless Bid*, the title of my first book, would be enough to convince you of that, and even as an oil trader in my 22-year career on the floor, I was far more comfortable being 'long' oil as opposed to being 'short.' My biases for oil's consistent rise in price, over the long haul, are deeply ingrained.

But it's also a logically ingrained conclusion. Costs of oil extraction continue to go up as conventional supplies of oil continue to decrease. Demand for oil continues to increase globally even as our domestic demand is beginning to wane. Oil prices that are in late 2014 and early 2015 below $60 a barrel are simply not going to last.

You'll never find a better time to institute a gas tax than right now.

As prices hovered near $4½ and $5 a gallon, drivers might have suffered, but we still saw strong economic growth, making it clear that our economy can thrive even when gasoline is much more expensive. But in 2015, with prices for gas under $3 a gallon, a 50¢ gas tax would be barely noticed.

My reason for a gas tax is focused: the proceeds should be directed entirely into development and integration towards renewable energy sources, including the incentivization of conversion to natural gas from oil. High oil prices are a prerequisite today for making natural gas and completely renewable sources economically viable in the market—while oil stocks have obviously swooned during the shale bust, solar stocks have fared even worse. And while the oil industry will make its way through the latest bust cycle, we can't be as dispassionate about renewables, since we ultimately need them to succeed. The U.S. government has a long history of helping to move us through transitions in energy, with incentives for coal when we depended on wood for heat in the 19th Century, when the move for oil was made in the beginnings of the 20th, and even today with the huge subsidies still being paid to big oil as incentives for development. It's time to refocus that support into renewables in the same way, and a gas tax would be a terrific way to start to do it.

Yes, the political roadblocks would be difficult to overcome. The Keystone XL pipeline argument has become a ridiculous proxy for the environmentalist lobby's complete disdain of the oil companies and a very pro-business U.S. energy policy Equally, the irrelevant case of Solyndra became the headline for the 'uselessness' of government incentives for renewable technology development. We should expect to see all the partisan dumbness this country can so easily muster on both sides when a gas tax to support renewable energy development is introduced. No matter. Its time has come, and I hope the next President of the United States has the courage to at least suggest it and force a discussion. Our current one clearly doesn't.

Finally, a concluding thought on the subtitle of this book, *The Myth of Saudi America*. Besides hopefully clearing up the faulty logic of striving to both become independent of oil imports and using our oil largesse as a political or economic hammer, I hope I've done one better. I hope I've proven that energy independence is not a goal even really worth pursuing. I think I've shown not only that the economics of U.S. shale prevent the U.S. from ever achieving a lasting independence from cheaper oil sources. Oil from shale has firmly taken on the role of a 'marginal barrel' source and therefore will be at the whim of the markets. No matter how we slice it, the U.S. is never going to be 'Saudi America,' with the ability to control the global oil markets in the way that a cheap and prolific per barrel producer like Saudi Arabia can.

But I would also argue that that is a very good thing, too. The Saudis represent the very essence of the Petro-state: they are entirely dependent on their oil revenues to support their economy and their people. Their politics

SHALE BOOM_ SHALE BUST

and policies are restricted solely based on the present and future price of oil and gas. Can anyone in power in Saudi Arabia ever take a moment to consider the future of our planet as it relates to the burning of carbon?

Look at Russia for another example of oil's terrible influence: Russia's ever-growing power of the dictator Vladimir Putin is, in my mind, a direct result of the state-owned (and therefore his) control of the Russian oil fields. The money that flows from those fields runs straight into the waiting hands of Putin's appointed oligarchs, any of whom would be crazy not to support the whims of the dictator in any way his heart desires, whether in Ukraine or Syria or on any other internal issue. Any opposition to the dictator is dealt with in the manner of former Yukos head Mikhail Khardakovsky, who spent 10 years in a cage in a Russian prison before being released on the eve of the 2014 Sochi Olympics as little more than a public relations stunt. Or perhaps like Boris Nemtsov, you could be gunned down in cold blood within steps of the Kremlin. Putin dictates who controls the oil, and in Russia (as with any true petro-state), that is all that matters.

This is what petro-states are like, and a very positive takeaway about the myth of Saudi America is that the U.S.A is not in the position to challenge to become one. The U.S. will not be the next Saudi Arabia or Russia. That's good news.

Instead, we've got this wonderful opportunity to still be a major producer of domestic oil that can benefit U.S. consumers and U.S. businesses alike, without losing sight of the ultimate goals of strengthening our economy, our people, and our future—in an environmentally responsible way.

Instead of an energy-independent America, that is the future I believe is really worth pursuing.

Addendum:
Boom Bust Investing

This is a chapter I didn't want to write—and then I thought that I absolutely should. My online readers seek investment advice from me three times a week, so even if I wanted to write a more durable book than a mere investment thesis, it would be wrong not to give at least some insight into where "Shale Boom, Shale Bust" leaves energy investors.

Betting on the price of oil is something I did for 25 years of my life, and I only came to use that knowledge to try and 'game' oil stocks much later. But if you're an individual investor, betting on the price of oil is precisely that: a bet. In no way can I advocate trying to trade oil as a part of a well-positioned investment strategy. Take it from a 25-year veteran of oil: you're not going to win. Yes, an investment in an index of commodity prices, like the Goldman Sachs Commodity Index (GSCI) can, at times, be a useful diversifier of a well-balanced portfolio. But an individual investor who wants to play the trajectory of oil prices is far more likely to succeed by using oil stocks as opposed to the price of the commodity itself. In fact, I have mostly abandoned oil futures in recent years to concentrate on the stocks myself.

Trust me, you'll live longer. And your money will, too.

Oil stocks are hardly a coward's way of investing, to be sure: in times when oil's price remains bullish, there are opportunities to often double or even triple one's money in oil stocks. In late 2014, we saw the downside of oil stocks, where many of the more speculative and highly leveraged shale producers lost more than 50% of their market caps. But don't forget that many of the names of now-underperforming exploration and production stocks were huge winners for their shareholders first.

For example, take Continental Resources, one of the largest independent shale oil producers in the Bakken. In late 2010, shares of Continental were selling for slightly more than $20; by mid-2014, you could have sold them for more than $80. Diamondback Energy, one of the smaller independents in the very, very hot Permian shale, had an even more stellar run: investors who bought it for $20 a share when the company was just a start-up in early 2013 could have taken a $70-a-share profit no more than 18 months later. Both of these have dropped 50% from their highs in the summer of 2014, but not before making shareholders a lot of money first. The downside seems very steep now, but the upside potential was even steeper.

With this in mind, you'd get to the end of my book on the shale boom and bust and read this Addendum expecting some ideas for the upcoming boom cycle I am predicting. I do have a few.

In my mind, there are three ways to strategically position oneself for what I think will be a new boom cycle in oil, one that I truly believe will see oil prices make an all-time new high above $150 a barrel. Let's look each of these ideas one at a time, as each opportunity is dependent on one's risk appetite and time horizons.

1. Investing in Exploration and Production 'Survivors'

I've laid out the scenario as I think it will progress with U.S. shale players. With continuing austerity in exploration budgets, a slashing of anything less than the most efficient and productive projects and a continued cash flow problem in servicing huge amounts of very high-interest debt, there's going to be quite a lot of reorganization, recapitalization, and outright contraction in the number of shale producers. There will also be a sure contraction in the total production of shale oil here in the U.S. Forget about Pioneer Natural Resources CEO Scott Sheffield's prediction of 14 million barrels a day of U.S. production; we'll more likely see 8-½ million or 8 million barrels a day first.

But as production targets get missed in reality as opposed to just in theory, we're going to see some of the players who were better capitalized and did not need to produce haphazardly during the downturn emerge as the strong survivors of the long oil 'winter.' Two companies come to mind immediately as personal favorites, although several could be considered candidates.

One is Cimarex (XEC), which has crafted itself into a stellar Permian shale specialist. Cimarex is a restructured natural gas company, which got the 'religion' of shale in the Permian basin only in late 2011. [Cimarex was hardly the first to realize the great potential of shale oil in this acreage it was already working. The true trailblazer in the Permian shale belongs to Pioneer Natural Resources (PXD) and Scott Sheffield.] But since refocusing to produce more oil and natural gas liquids, Cimarex has done the Permian shale region in 'the right way'—that is, not moving too quickly or drilling at every opportunity, but slowly converting to a far more 'oily' E+P. Even now, Cimarex's production is only 30% oil, yet its revenues from shale oil are more than 50% of its total. Moreover, the company has done this astoundingly without anywhere near the kind of precarious leverage that plagues almost all other players in the space. With about a half billion in cash and a total liability of about $1.5B and an approximate EBITDA of $750m, it has a very strong leverage ratio of 1.5 times. Cimarex will not be one of the first companies to break under the strain of low oil prices; it will be one of the last.

When looking for 'survivors' of what is likely to be an extended period of sub-$75 oil, this is precisely what we want to see: a tremendous potential for continued development, like in the hot Permian, and a financial structure that will definitely see them through to the next cycle upturn. Finding an oil company with these two strong attributes is pretty rare. Unfortunately for us, however, pretty much all of the analysts have seen the same value in Cimarex as I have, so shares are currently overpriced for the company's potential, but it still remains one of the best I see in the space. If there was a 'conservative' beta-play in U.S. shale to recommend, it's Cimarex.

Another E+P with perhaps even more to recommend is most likely not nearly as overpriced: EOG Resources. EOG's previous CEO, Mark Papa, was a true maverick in shale oil, expanding early and finding quality acreage first in the Bakken, then in the mid-Texas Eagle Ford Shale, and finally in the Wolfcamp area of the Permian basin in West Texas. Well results since 2010 have had a consistently upward trajectory, as do well efficiencies, overall production volumes, dropping transport costs, and recovery rates. With prime acreage in the three hottest U.S. oil shale plays, EOG has the kind of flexibility that other U.S. E+Ps can only dream of.

Because of its high margins and optionality, EOG is the perfect U.S. shale oil E+P. While other oil companies must increase production to survive a downturn in oil prices just to service debt and keep the cash flowing, EOG's low cost of recovery allows it to skate happily forward at even low $40's crude prices. It is one of the few shale players that could turn up the spigot without panic and wait for the turnaround with no risk of default or bankruptcy. Instead, the company proved it was smarter than that. At a time when others were scrambling to increase production, EOG chose in early 2015 to slash its spending a monumental 40% and cut drilling and production as well, guiding for a lower production rate for 2015—and purposefully missing earnings projections for the first time in 2 ½ years.

Simply put, CEO Bill Thomas chose not to chase the earnings game at the worst time, counting on a natural selection and weeding out of weaker shale players, and planning on producing oil only when better market conditions returned. Wall Street may not like that…but I do. The decision for EOG to 'keep its powder dry' until oil prices turn north is in direct contrast to almost everyone else in the space. EOG's increase in deferred inventory means it is spending money to keep wells online but not produce, meaning that when prices are advantageous, EOG can be very fast to take advantage while others will be scrambling. That's smart.

EOG and Cimarex represent my best ideas in E+Ps.

2. Investing in Pipeline Companies

Another way to play the coming boom cycle is in infrastructure, particularly pipelines. The oil and gas pipeline world was changed by Richard Kinder, CEO of Kinder Morgan, when he pioneered using the brilliant tax-advantaged structure of Master Limited Partnership (MLP) for his newly formed pipeline company in 1997. By nature, an MLP is forced to distribute most all of its profits to its 'partners,' so growing a pipeline MLP always depends on the strength of one's borrowing power. By constantly restructuring debt and increasing acquisitions, MLPs can grow rapidly without many of the tax consequences of a regular C corporation.

And Kinder did grow, buying out KN energy, which included Natural Gas Pipeline Corporation of America, in 1999. In 2005, KMI paid $5.6b for Canada pipeline giant Terasen. In 2012, Kinder acquired the massive El Paso network for $38b. Kinder's model has been copied by dozens of others, and today almost every pipeline company is structured as an MLP.

Then, in August of 2014, for seemingly no reason, Kinder chose to restructure his four companies back into one old-fashioned C corporation. One can only guess whether he saw the collapse in crude oil coming, but the move could not have been better timed. The distress in shale oil has caused an equal distress in oil and gas financing, and a medium-term contraction in infrastructure buildouts, an absolute necessity for pipeline MLPs. If you're an MLP, you have to constantly grow, or ultimately die, as your old pipes grow less and less profitable along with the naturally decaying acreage they are servicing.

But as a newly formed C corporation, Kinder is now able to generate independent cash flow and access debt markets without the MLP overhang of obligatory distributions. The brilliance of the move was seen in his fire-sale acquisition of Hiland Partners in January 2015 for $3b. This sale of pipes owned mostly by Continental Resources CEO Harold Hamm moves Rich Kinder into the Bakken precisely at the time when production is about to sag and infrastructure assets are about to be put up for sale at 'opportunistic' prices.

One more example of this consolidation was Energy Transfer Partners' (ETP) $18b buyout of Regency Partners' (RGP) Eagle Ford and Permian transport assets. More of these sales are going to have to happen, and KMI is uniquely positioned in the space to be one to do a lot more of them. To put it simply, Rich Kinder always manages to be at the right place at the right time. For this reason alone, KMI is the one pipeline company I tend to recommend in 2015 for the long haul, waiting on the inevitable upturn in oil prices.

3. Investing in the Cash-Rich and Opportunistic

Finally, one could invest in other "vultures" who are preparing to pick over the bones of a cracking shale oil industry. As of March 2015, several oil and gas conferences have taken place with outwardly non-panicked attendees. "Keep calm and frack on" was the theme of Keybank Capital's presentation at the North American Prospect Expo in February 2015, and indeed, the openly available oil assets that were being shopped were decidedly uninteresting and non-core, unlikely to attract any good offers. But that's likely going to change. Whiting Petroleum (WLL), after unsuccessfully seeking a buyer, announced it would sell $1B in assets in 2015, and it won't be alone. Sales will ultimately be necessary to ensure survival, and the longer prices stay depressed, the more desperate the sellers will have to become.

Into this scramble for capital to survive march the vultures: those with ready cash capable of picking up assets and waiting for a more advantageous moment to develop and profit from them. Two sub-groups of circling opportunistic feeders come to mind: private equity firms and major integrated oil companies.

We've talked about the role that private equity is likely to play in the coming reorganization of oil production here in the U.S. There is literally a who's who of PE firms that have raised huge fund resources for the sole purpose of buying oil assets and distressed paper: Carlyle Group, Warburg Pincus, Tudor Pickering, Apollo Global Management, KKR, and others, but the one that always seems to do just that much better in these sector-wide free-for-alls (and is also publicly traded) is Blackstone (BX). When the legendary Steve Schwarzman's firm went public in 2007, I was convinced that this was merely an opportunity to take advantage of a huge spike in the stock market for the partners in Blackstone to cash out and ultimately call it a day. I saw the public offering then as an unworthy investment, which could only serve to fill the partners' pockets while they proceeded to 'mail it in' for their new shareholders. But I have been proven completely wrong. Blackstone's history since its public offering is a continued history of success stories, and I believe the current energy restructuring opportunity will be no different. Elsewhere in this book, I talk a bit about the deal it made with Linn Energy, with very advantageous terms for Blackstone. As a long-term hold, I can find no better (public) PE firm to invest in.

I've also written here a bit about integrated mega-cap oil and its role in the coming reorganization. Already, Royal Dutch Shell has made what I think will be its 'big move' in M&A with the acquisition of British natural gas and LNG specialist BG Group. That deal proves that just because you're in the market for assets to buy doesn't mean that a terrific deal necessarily will become available—even though the RDS-BG merger represents big dollars and huge future potential for growth, it isn't immediately accretive and in fact may never be unless natural gas stages a major rally in the next decade. But I believe that Exxon Mobil (XOM) is in by far the best position to get a blockbuster deal done that will be at value and incredibly accretive over several decades, much like the buy of Mobil oil accomplished in the 90s. Its list of possible candidates is practically limitless and yet, it has the added caution of its mistimed buy of natural gas producer XTO Energy in 2009. This time around, I believe Exxon's focus will be on crude- and liquids-focused U.S. shale players that have very deep assets that would yield decades of production growth. The list for players like this is actually quite short and includes Anadarko Petroleum (APC), Hess (HES), Continental Resources (CLR), and perhaps a few others.

But no matter who the ultimate target is, I'd much rather bet on the company with the money, patience, and long-term outlook to benefit from a buyout of a major shale player than try to guess at the company that is going to get bought. In this, I still find Exxon-Mobil to be the best long-term play among the majors for taking advantage of the shale bust—and ultimate next boom.

Despite the swoon that has overcome the oil sector since the bust began in late 2014, these three sub-sectors continue to deliver the best long-term opportunity in energy. Finding the right survivor, infrastructure provider, and winning vulture are three strategies to take advantage of the current, yet temporary, depressed oil and energy stock prices.

Index

About the Author

Dan Dicker had more than 20 years' experience on the floor of the New York Mercantile Exchange, where he traded crude oil, natural gas, unleaded gasoline, and heating oil futures contracts for his own accounts. His previous book, *Oil's Endless Bid: Taming the Unreliable Price of Oil to Secure Our Economy*, was published by John Wiley & Sons in 2011 and was named one of that year's Best Business Books by both *Bloomberg BusinessWeek* and *Library Journal.*

Dan is currently President and partner of MercBloc LLC, a wealth management firm, as well as a senior contributor at Jim Cramer's TheStreet. com, where he writes on energy markets and investing in the energy space. He has lent his expertise as an oil markets analyst in hundreds of live radio and television broadcasts on CNBC, Bloomberg, MSNBC, CNN, NBC Nightly News, CNN and Yahoo Finance among others. Dan lives with his wife and family in New York.

12812685R00069

Printed in Great Britain
by Amazon.co.uk, Ltd.,
Marston Gate.